THE FORMAL GARDEN
IN ENGLAND

·THE·
·FORMAL· GARDEN·
·IN ·ENGLAND·
·BY ·REGINALD·BLOMFIELD·
·AND ·F·INIGO·THOMAS·

WATERSTONE · LONDON

This edition published by
Waterstone & Co. Limited in 1985.

First published in 1892.
Copyright © The Estate of Reginald Blomfield.

Cover Design by Peter Ward.

Printed and bound in Great Britain
by Richard Clay (The Chaucer Press) Ltd,
Bungay, Suffolk

Distributed (except in the USA) by
Thames and Hudson Ltd.

ISBN 0 947752 36 6

FOREWORD

This reprint of Sir Reginald Blomfield's classic on the design of the formal garden is particularly appropriate in view of the current reawakening of interest in the formal method. With few exceptions informality of an increasingly degenerate kind has been in the ascendancy in garden design in this country at least since the war. A design manual and historical survey of this kind is sorely needed.

When first published in 1892 the book was also something of a pioneer and proselytiser. It reacted against both the mindless geometry of Victorian bedding-out and against the equally woolly though more fashionable *naturalism* of William Robinson and his school. The basic thesis of the work is that the garden should be a logical extension of the house, reflecting its geometry and style, so that it becomes a series of linked *rooms* and spaces of various function and orientation. This is in direct contrast to the approach of the landscape school where the form of the garden is primarily a response to the site and a foil to the architecture.

FOREWORD

One of the periodic controversies which span the history of taste in gardening was sparked off by the book, and it was quite as vitriolic a row as these affairs usually are. William Robinson published an article on Blomfield in July 1892 under the title *Garden Design and Architects' Gardens* and Blomfield almost immediately replied in print in a lengthy preface to the second edition of his book in October 1892.

Although Blomfield's practice was mainly concerned with large country houses (he remodelled Chequers and Mellerstain for example), the ideas propounded in this book are equally applicable on the much contracted scale of today's gardens, even to the smallest town garden.

Blomfield begins by giving us a highly readable history of gardening in England and an account of the literature. He concentrates, and this is the value of the work, on design rather than horticulture. While ignoring cultural directions, however, he does give very useful lists of early plants and the manner of their use. The range of his enthusiasm is surprising; he can admire, for instance, the decorative prettiness of an Elizabethan knot as much as the cool simplicity of an early eighteenth-century *par terre a l'Anglais*.

The latter part of the book deals in greater detail with the individual elements of the formal garden; the whole illustrated by delightful early engravings and by the drawings of H Inigo Thomas, himself a garden designer of the formal school.

FOREWORD

The book is full of inspiring ideas and design readily adaptable to today's gardens. There are knots, par terres, arbours, pleached alleys and topiary specimens as well as the earthworks and hardware: mounts, summerhouses, gates, carpenters' work, vases – the list is endless. The degree of elaboration and upkeep involved in these schemes ranges from the prohibitively costly to wonderfully simple effects which would be within everyone's reach. The book conjures up stunning visions which one can only wonder are not more generally attempted.

CONTENTS

CHAPTER I

CHAPTER VII

CHAPTER VIII

CHAPTER IX

CHAPTER X

ILLUSTRATIONS

CHAPTER I

THE FORMAL METHOD AND THE LANDSCAPE GARDENER

THE Formal System of Gardening has suffered from a question-begging name. It has been labelled "Formal" by its ill-wishers; and though, in a way, the term expresses the orderly result at which the system aims, the implied reproach is disingenuous. The history of this method of dealing with gardens will be discussed in subsequent chapters, but as some misunderstanding prevails as to its intention, and any quantity of misrepresentation, it will be well to clear the ground by a statement of the principles and standpoint of the Formal School as compared with Landscape Gardening.

The question at issue is a very simple one. Is the garden to be considered in relation to the house, and as an integral part of a design which depends for its success on the combined effect of house and garden; or is the house to be ignored in dealing with the garden? The latter is the

position of the landscape gardener in real fact.
There is some affectation in his treatises of
recognising the relationship between the two,
but his actual practice shows that this admission
is only borrowed from the formal school to
save appearances, and is out of court in a
method which systematically dispenses with
any kind of system whatever.

The formal treatment of gardens ought,
perhaps, to be called the architectural treatment
of gardens, for it consists in the extension of the
principles of design which govern the house to
the grounds which surround it.   Architects are
often abused for ignoring the surroundings of
their buildings in towns, and under conditions
which make it impossible for them to do otherwise ; but if the reproach has force, and it
certainly has, it applies with greater justice to
those who control both the house and its surroundings, and yet deliberately set the two at
variance.   The object of formal gardening is to
bring the two into harmony, to make the house
grow out of its surroundings, and to prevent its
being an excrescence on the face of nature.   The
building cannot resemble anything in nature.
unless you are content with a mud-hut and
cover it with grass.   Architecture in any shape
has certain definite characteristics which it
cannot get rid of ; but, on the other hand, you
can lay out the grounds, and alter the levels,
and plant hedges and trees exactly as you

please ; in a word, you can so control and modify the grounds as to bring nature into harmony with the house, if you cannot bring the house into harmony with nature. The harmony arrived at is not any trick of imitation, but an affair of a dominant idea which stamps its impress on house and grounds alike.

Starting, then, with the house as our datum, we have to consider it as a visible object, what sort of thing it is that we are actually looking at. A house, or any other building, considered simply as a visible object, presents to the eye certain masses arranged in definite planes and proportions, and certain colours distributed in definite quality and quantity. It is regular, it presents straight lines and geometrical curves. Any but the most ill-considered efforts in building—anything with any title to the name of architecture—implies premeditated form in accordance with certain limits and necessities. However picturesque the result, however bravely some chimney breaks the sky-line, or some gable contradicts another, all architecture implies restraint, and if not symmetry, at least balance. There is order everywhere and there is no escaping it. Now, suppose this visible object dropped, let us say from heaven, into the middle of a piece of ground, and this piece of ground laid out with a studied avoidance of all order, all balance, all definite lines, and the result must be a hopeless disagreement between the house and its surroundings. This very effect can be seen in the efforts of the landscape gardener, and in old country houses, such as Barrington Court, near Langport, where the gardens have not been kept up. There is a gaunt, famished, incomplete look about these houses, which is due quite as much to the obvious want of relation between the house and its grounds, as to any associations of decay.

Something, then, of the quality of the house must be found in the grounds. The house will have its regular approach and its courtyard— rectangular, round, or oval—its terrace, its paths straight and wide, its broad masses of unbroken grass, its trimmed hedges and alleys, its flower-beds bounded by the strong definite lines of box-edgings and the like—all will show the quality of order and restraint ; the motive of the house suggests itself in the terrace and the gazebo, and recurs, like the theme in a coda, as you pass between the piers of the garden gate.

Thus the formal garden will produce with the house a homogeneous result, which cannot be reached by either singly. Now let us see how the landscape gardener deals with the problem of house and grounds.

It is not easy to state his principles, for his system consists in the absence of any ; and most modern writers on the subject lead off with hearty and indiscriminate abuse of formal gardening, after which they incontinently drop the question of garden design, and go off at a tangent on horticulture and hot-houses.   A great deal is said about nature and her beauty, and fidelity to nature, and so on ; but as the landscape gardener never takes the trouble to state precisely what he means by nature, and indeed prefers to use the word in half a dozen different senses, we are not very much the wiser so far as principles are concerned.   The axiom on which the system rests is this—" Whatever nature does is right ; therefore let us go and copy her."   Let us obliterate the marks of man's handiwork (and particularly any suspicion of that bad man, the architect), and though we shall manipulate the face of nature with the greatest freedom, we shall be careful to make people believe that we have not manipulated it at all.   Various rules are given as to the proper method of " copying nature's graceful touch " —the favourite phrase of the landscapist.   The older writers, such as Wheatly (*Observations on Modern Gardening*, 1770), had a theory which was at least intelligible as a theory.   They considered the landscape gardener as a painter on a colossal scale.   By altering natural scenery he was to produce such landscapes as are admired in the works of the old masters.   The method of procedure as explained by Wheatly is this. You determine *à priori* the abstract characteristics of any natural object ; and then, on considerations evolved from your inner con-

sciousness, you alter the surrounding scenery to
bring out these characteristics. For instance,
the characteristics of rocks are determined to
be " dignity, terror, and fancy." By way of
enhancing dignity, Wheatly tells us to cut away
the ground to make them steeper ; and to
refine their appearance we are to cover them
up with " shrubby and creeping plants." Or
again, if the scenery is wild, we may make
it wilder by making a ruined stone bridge.
Straight lines and unbroken masses of foliage
are to be avoided at all costs, in order to secure
variety of effect, " and the planter is to plant
trees of different foliage at stated intervals, by
way of reproducing the colours of the painter's
palette." These views are repeated in modern
treatises on landscape gardening, with, however,
a curious inversion. Wheatly's idea was that
we should saturate our minds with the compositions of the old masters, and then proceed to
alter actual scenery till it resembled their
pictures ; but the modern landscapist tells us
that we are to copy nature—that is, study a
piece of scenery of natural formation, and
then reproduce this in our gardens. Wheatly
admitted design of some sort, while his suc-
cessors direct every effort to imitating the
absence of design. The latter insist that we
are not to copy nature literally, but only in her
spirit, whatever that may mean. Mr. Robinson
says, " We should compose from nature as land-

scape artists do. It is still his (the landscape gardener's) privilege to make ever-changing pictures out of nature's own material—sky and trees, water and flowers and grass. If he would not prefer this to painting in pigments, he has no business to be a landscape gardener. The aim should be never to rest till the garden is a reflex of nature in her fairest moods." For instance, because nature is assumed never to show straight lines, all paths are to be made crooked, and presumably Mr. Robinson's dictum that " walks should be concealed as much as possible, and reduced to the most modest dimensions" is based on the state of a virgin forest ; the argument perhaps running thus, because in a virgin forest there are no paths at all, let us in our acre and a half of garden make as little of the paths as possible. Deception is a prim-ary object of the landscape gardener. Thus to get variety, and to deceive the eye into sup-posing that the garden is larger than it is, the paths are to wind about in all directions, and the lawns are not to be left in broad expanse, but dotted about with pampas grasses, foreign shrubs, or anything else that will break up the surface. As was said by a witty Frenchman, " Rien n'est plus facile que de dessiner un parc anglais ; on n'a qu'à enivrer son jardinier, et à suivre son trace."

Mr. Milner, a recent writer on landscape gardening, has the courage to define what he calls his art : "The art of landscape gardening may be stated as the taking true cognisance of nature's means for the expression of beauty, and so disposing those means artistically as to co-operate for our delight in given conditions." This is a hard saying, put in plain English it seems to amount to this : Select such landscape effects as appear to you to be beautiful, and endeavour to reproduce them in your garden. The process suggests the paste-pot and scissors of the penny-a-liner. By observation of natural scenery the landscape gardener is to form certain generalisations to guide his practice. Here are some of the results of Mr. Milner's studies : " A calculated shadow on a lawn is a resource of value for the artistic use of natural effect. In every situation a beyond implies discovery and affects the imagination ; the area is circumscribed of which we can take cognisance too readily and completely ; imagination is then confused or frustrated. The beauty of water, in motion or still, is of universal acceptance. The created character of a water feature must be consonant with the surrounding land, for fitness to surrounding conditions is a measure of beauty to both ; a lake expresses spaciousness, but much of its charm is due to its outline." There is a curious irrelevance about these apothegms which reminds one of Ollendorf : " My aunt is beautiful, but have you seen my sister's cat ? "

As to any system, Mr. Milner throws up the

sponge at once. He admits in his first chapter
that landscape gardening can have no set of
fixed principles. He says generally that we are
not to copy nature, but "to adapt and garner
her beauties." Yet his advice as to treatment
of details is point-blank copy. "The lawn of
our garden" should present the appearance of a
"grassy glade in a wood," appear, in short, to
be exactly what it is not. For this is another of
the objects of the landscape gardener; his aim
is not to show things as they are, but as they
are not. His first ambition is to make his
interference with nature look "natural-like";
his second, to produce a false impression on the
spectator and make him think the grounds to
be twice as big as they are. "Bridges may be
contrived to excite the impression of length."
"The removal of some (trees) in particular
situations, with a coincident lowering of the
bank, will give an effect of lengthening the
water area." So in regard to trees, "a hill is
made to appear higher if its summit be planted."
Or again, "an enclosure pure and simple, even
though it be of leaves and not a brick wall,
gives a shut-in and cramped feeling which need-
lessly militates against expressions of beauty and
expanse that may be deftly gained from outside
the boundary lines,"—that is, by deftly cutting
holes in the line of trees we lead people to
suppose that our neighbour's estate belongs to
us. Hitherto no mention has been made of

architecture in this description of landscape gardening. Indeed, it is the object of the landscape gardener to exclude the architect from the garden, for he feels, like Demetrius, the silversmith, that his craft is in danger to be set at naught; and having succeeded in expelling the architect a hundred and fifty years ago, he is naturally unwilling to let him in again. Mr. Milner does point out that the house should stand on a terrace, but proceeds to stultify his own admission by stating that the terrace "differs from the garden proper, which, though fine in calculated detail of its plan, should express by its breadth of treatment most unmistakably that nature has triumphed over art, because art has subtly tutored the development of nature," which, if it means anything, must mean that when you enter the garden you are to leave all thought of architecture behind you.

Thus, the substantial difference between the two views of gardening is this. The formal school insists upon design; the house and the grounds should be designed together and in relation to each other; no attempt should be made to conceal the design of the garden, there being no reason for doing so, but the bounding lines, whether it is the garden wall or the lines of paths and parterres, should be shown frankly and unreservedly, and the garden will be treated specifically as an enclosed space to be laid out exactly as the designer pleases. The landscape gardener, on the other hand, turns his back upon architecture at the earliest opportunity and devotes his energies to making the garden suggest natural scenery, to giving a false impression as to its size by sedulously concealing all boundary lines, and to modifying the scenery beyond the garden itself, by planting or cutting down trees, as may be necessary to what he calls his picture. In matters of taste there is no arguing with a man. Probably people with a feeling for design and order will prefer the formal garden, while the landscape system, as it requires no knowledge of design, appeals to the average person who " knows what he likes," if he does not know anything else.

One or ·two charges, however, which have been brought against the formal system, ought to be dealt with here. In the first place, it is said to be unnatural to lay out a garden in straight lines and regular banks and to clip your hedges. The landscape gardener appears to suppose that he has a monopoly of nature. Now, what is "nature" and what is "natural" in relation to gardens? "Il faut se méfier du mirage de le mot ' naturel ' lorsqu'il s'agit des nuances de la sensibilité. Outre qu'il sert de masque, le plus souvent, aux inintelligences des ignorants ou aux hostilités des gens vulgaires, il a le malheur de ne pas envelopper de signification précise au regard du philosophe." [1]

[1] Paul Bourget.

" Nature " must mean the earth itself and the forces at work in the earth, and the waters of the earth and sky, and the trees, flowers, and grass which grow on the earth, no matter whether planted by man or not. A clipped yew-tree is as much a part of nature—that is, subject to natural laws, as a forest oak ; but the landscapist, by appealing to associations which surround the personification of nature, holds up the clipped yew - tree to obloquy as something against nature.   So far as that goes, it is no more unnatural to clip a yew-tree than to cut grass. Again, " nature " is said to prefer a curved line to a straight, and it is thence inferred that all the lines in a garden, and especially paths, should be curved.   Now as a matter of fact in nature— that is, in the visible phenomena of the earth's surface—there are no lines at all ; " a line " is simply an abstraction which conveniently expresses the direction of a succession of objects which   may   be   either   straight   or   curved. " Nature " has nothing to do with either straight lines or curved ; it is simply begging the question to lay it down as an axiom that curved lines are more " natural " than straight. As a matter of fact, whatever " naturalness " there may be about it applies quite as well to a straight path and a plain expanse of grass ; and it is open to us to say that the natural man would probably prefer a straight path to a zigzag, and that when his eye seeks wearily for the rest of some quiet breadth of lawn and the welcome finality of a wall or hedgerow, he is " naturally " bored by the landscapist with his curves and his clumps.

The word " natural " can only mean something belonging to nature, or something done in accordance with nature's laws, as, for instance, planting a tree with its roots underground instead of upside down ; but when the landscapist uses the word " natural," as when he calls his system a "purely artistic and natural " style, he means by it a style which imitates the visible results of natural causes, as, for instance, the copy of a piece of natural rock in a rockery. Now there is nothing more natural, properly speaking, about this than there is in the formation of a grass bank in the shape of a horse-shoe. In fact, this vaunted naturalness of landscape gardening is a sham ; instead of leaving nature alone, the landscapist is always struggling to make nature lend itself to his deceptions.   Mr. Milner gives unconsciously two instances of this.   In a chapter on " Public Parks and Cemeteries " he tells us how, at Preston, a railway embankment, which runs across the public park, was made to look quite natural by " planting and irregular lines of walk and turf.   Rockwork even has been introduced to foster the idea that the towering mass is only one part of an old cliff."   And at Glossop the landscape gardener was still more heroic.

The park was divided by a ravine, with a stream running along the bottom. Accordingly, " the beautiful and natural parts of the ravine were picked out and made the most of, whilst, in order to convert the parts into a whole, the sides were in places levelled down, and the stream covered,"—a somewhat scurvy treatment of nature by the landscape gardener. This is all very well, but what becomes of nature ? As Sir Uvedale Price said of Brown and his clumps of trees, " While Mr. Brown was removing old pieces of formality, he was establishing new ones of a more extensive and mischievous consequence." The claims of landscape gardening to be the true " natural style " will not bear investigation. When Addison and Pope sneered at the formal garden and praised "the amiable simplicity of unadorned nature," the logical conclusion would have been to condemn the garden altogether, and to let the house, if a house was to be allowed at all, rise from the heart of the thicket, or sheer from the rough hillside. It is hard to see how there is less interference with nature in an untidy grotto of shells and rocks than in a comfortable red-brick gazebo, and the entire extent of masonry used by Kent in his temples and grottoes at Stowe, must have been at least equal to the amount used by Le Nôtre at Sceaux or Chantilly. To suppose that love of nature is shown by trying to produce the effects of wild nature on a small scale in a garden is clearly absurd ; any one who loves natural scenery will want the real thing ; he will hardly be content to sit in his rockery and suppose himself to be among the mountains. And again, some loyalty to her methods might have been expected of these enthusiasts for nature. It is surely flying in the face of nature to fill the garden with tropical plants, as we are urged to do by the writers on Landscape Gardening, ignoring the entire difference of climate, and the fact that a colour which may look superb in the midst of other strong colours, will look gaudy and vulgar amongst our sober tints, and that a leaf like that of the yucca, which may be all very well in its own country, is out of scale and character amidst the modest foliage of English trees. The formal gardener is, by his principles, entitled to do what he likes with nature, but the landscapist gets involved in all sorts of contradictions. He " copies nature's graceful touch," but under totally different conditions to the original ; so far, therefore, from being loyal to nature, he is engaged in a perpetual struggle to prove her an ass. When we find him talking of " quite second-rate types of vegetation " (Mr. Robinson), and finding fault with nature for having put a running stream like the Derwent among rocks instead of " a more temperate river " (Wheatly), we begin to suspect that his " truth "

is a mere convention.   Sainte-Beuve said of the
Abbé Delille that he sincerely believed in his
love of the fields, " c'était la mode de la nature,
on admirait la campagne du sein des boudoirs."
Our landscape gardeners take themselves too
seriously ; as the late Charles Blanc pointed out,
their pretensions to be natural have landed them
in the worst of all vices—" le faux naturel."

Two other charges are brought against the
formal garden : first, that it involves much
building and statuary ; secondly, that it requires
much space.   Neither the one nor the other
is more necessary to the English formal garden
than it is to the landscape garden.   In regard
to the first, Mr. Milner gives some very remarkable designs of rustic boat-houses, and summerhouses, and porticoes, as part and parcel of the
landscape garden ; and it will appear that the
wholesale and immoderate use of temples,
statues, grottoes, made ruins, broken bridges
and the like, originated with the landscape
gardener, not with the formal school.   In point
of fact, though statuary was used in the old
English garden, it was used much less than in
the French and Italian gardens.   Those who
attack the old English formal garden do not
take the trouble to master its very considerable
difference from the continental gardens of the
same period.   They seem to consider the
English Renaissance as identical with the
Italian, and the public, seeing such dismal

fiascoes in the Italian style as the Crystal
Palace Gardens and the basin at the head of
the Serpentine, confuse these with the old
English garden in one wholesale condemnation
of the formal style. Against the introduction
of the formal Italian garden of the sixteenth
century into England there is a very great deal
to be said. Such a garden properly carried
out would be immensely costly, unless the
balustrades and ornaments were made in composition, which is sure to come to pieces in a
very few years, and in any case never colours
(the case, by the way, with several of the most
famous Italian gardens). Moreover, our climate
and the quality of light in England make it
impossible to obtain the effect which is actually
attained in the great Italian gardens, such as
those at Tivoli. The older English garden, as
I shall show later, was by no means a direct copy
of the Italian ; and as to the matter of space, it
is a mere assumption to lay it down that the
formal style in England requires a great expanse
of ground to be seen to perfection. This
was necessary, no doubt, in the old French
garden, but not in the English. Some of the
best examples are on a comparatively small
scale. The gardens at Haddon Hall are in
three stages—the two top terraces only measure
about 70 paces by 18 wide apiece, and the
lower garden is only about 40 paces square.
The beautiful old garden at Brickwall, in

Sussex, all walled in, measures about 65 paces by 55, and the kitchen and fruit garden about 90 by 50. The garden of Edzell Castle, in Forfarshire, all walled in, measures 58 paces long by 48 wide ; and a charming little flower garden

THE TERRACE : HADDON HALL : DERBYSHIRE 22

FIG. 1.—Haddon Hall.

at Stobhall, near Perth, in the old Scotch style is not much more than half an acre in extent. In fact, if either style wants room it is the land-scape, for unrestricted space is of the essence of natural scenery ; and, indeed, the only places in which its use appears reasonable are gardens such as those of Chatsworth, where the grounds are so large that there is a real suggestion of scenery

sui generis, as of a wood in which clearings have
been made and the grass kept carefully trimmed.

The word " garden " itself means an enclosed
space, a garth or yard surrounded by walls, as
opposed to unenclosed fields and woods. The
formal garden, with its insistence on strong
bounding lines, is, strictly speaking, the only
" garden " possible ; and it was not till the decay
of architecture, which began in the middle of
the eighteenth century, that any other method
of dealing with a garden was entertained.

Before quitting the subject of gardens in
general, a distinction should be laid down
between garden design and horticulture. The
landscape gardener treats of the two indis-
criminately, yet they are entirely distinct, and
it is evident that to plan out the general dis-
position of a garden the knowledge necessary is
that of design, not of the best method of growing a gigantic gooseberry. Mr. Robinson justly
remarks that " the profession of an architect
has no one thing in common with that of horticulture," and infers from this that the French
do wrong to give the control of the Luxembourg gardens to an architect. But the question
is not one of horticulture at all, but of design ;
and just as in the house, the designer is only
indirectly concerned with the process of manu-
facturing his bricks, so in the garden the designer need not know the best method of
planting every flower or shrub included in his

design ; the gardener should see to that. The horticulturist and the gardener are indispensable, but they should work under control, and they stand in the same relation to the designer as the artist's colourman does to the painter, or perhaps it would be fairer to say, as the builder and his workmen stand to the architect. The two ought to work together. The designer, whether professional or amateur, should lay down the main lines and deal with the garden as a whole, but the execution, such as the best method of forming beds, laying turf, planting trees, and pruning hedges, should be left to the gardener, whose proper business it is.

CHAPTER II

In his *Essay on Gardening* Horace Walpole says that we are " apt to think that Sir William Temple and King William introduced the formal style, but by the description of Lord Burleigh's gardens at Theobalds, and of those at Nonsuch, we find that the magnificent, though false taste was known here as early as the reigns of Henry VIII. and his daughter." This is of a piece with Walpole's generalisations on Gothic architecture. He seems to have supposed that it was possible to import an exotic style wholesale into the midst of a people with a strong indigenous tradition. As a matter of fact, the advance in garden design in the sixteenth century was, like English architecture of the time, the result of the grafting of ideas brought back from Italy on the vigorous stock of mediæval art, and the fully-developed formal garden of the seventeenth century retained features which were distinct survivals from the mediæval garden.

No instances remain of any mediæval garden, and we have to form our ideas of it chiefly from illuminated manuscripts and early paintings. They were walled in, and supplied with water in conduits and fountains, and planted closely with hedges and alleys, as appears from the well-known lines written by James I. of Scotland during his captivity at Windsor, 1405-1424.

> "Now was there made, fast by the Tower's wall,
> A garden fair, and in corneris set
> Ane herbere green with wandes long and small,
> Railit about, and so with treeis set,
> Was all the place, and hawthorn hedges knet
> Thet lyf was non, walking there forbye,
> That might therein scarce any wight espye—
> So thick the boughis and the leaves green
> Beshaded all the alleys that there were—
> And myddis every herbere might be seene
> The sharp, green, sweete junipere."

Mr. Hazlitt (*Gleanings in old Garden Literature*) has collected what evidence there is of the mediæval garden in contemporary literature, and unfortunately there is very little that throws much light on its arrangement. It was not, however, quite such an indiscriminate affair as Mr. Hazlitt suggests. In "The Romance of the Rose " in the British Museum (Harl. MS. 4425) there is a beautiful illumination of a garden, dating from the latter part of the fifteenth century. This garden is divided into two by a fence, with a high gateway in the middle, but both gardens are surrounded by a wall with battlements.   In the centre of

Fig. 2.—From " The Romance of the Rose."

the left-hand garden is a fountain or conduit of copper, standing in a circular basin with a marble curb, and a little runnel of water in a marble channel.   The right-hand garden shows rectangular grass plots, in one of which is an orange-tree in a circular fence ; at the farther end is a fence of flowers on a wooden trellis— and peacocks are shown in the garden. Both gardens are evidently pleasure or flower gardens, as distinct from the kitchen garden. Mr. Hazlitt suggests that "arbour" was originally "herbarium," a space of grass planted with trees ; but the lines quoted above certainly refer to a "green arbour," and prove that by the beginning of the fifteenth century an arbour, in pretty much the sense that we should understand it, formed a regular part of the garden. On page 14^B of "The Romance of the Rose" there is a drawing of a garden with a wall about 7 feet high with battlements. On page 25 there is a drawing of a feature which seems to have been common in the mediæval garden—a square embrasure was formed in the brickwork of the garden wall, with a seat round three sides about 2 feet wide and 18 inches above the ground ; the seat was of grass. On page 30 a bed of roses is shown instead of the grass seat ; on page 43 a green walk, such as is frequently referred to in old writers, is shown, formed on wooden framing with red and white roses.

It is not, however, till the time of Henry VIII. that we come across any specific facts as to the arrangement of gardens. In 1520 Cardinal Wolsey began his great palace of Hampton Court. Wolsey's gardens, as described by George Cavendish, resemble the picture given by James I.

Fig. 3.—From "The Romance of the Rose."

"My garden sweet, enclosed with walles strong,
Embanked with benches to sytt and take my rest,
The knottes so enknotted, it cannot be exprest,

> With arbours and allys so pleasant and so dulce,
> The pestilent ayres with flavors to repulse."

The enclosing walls, the knottes or figured flower-beds, the arbours and alleys, formed part of the mediæval gardens ; but when, after Wolsey's death in 1530, the palace and gardens came into the hands of Henry VIII. signs appear of a new influence at work. Statues and figures of all kinds were introduced, and various fantastic features which were, no doubt, borrowed from Italy. In the chapter - house accounts for the additions made by Henry VIII. appear the following entries :—

" Payd to Harry Corantt of Kyngston carver for making and entaylling of 38 of the kynges and queenys Beestes in freeston, baryng shyldes wyth the kynges armes and the queenys ; that is to say, foure dragones, scyx lyones, five grewhounds, five harttes, foure unicornes serving to stand about the ponddes in the pondyard at 26s. the piece, £49 : 8 : 0.

" Item for paynting of 30 stone bests standyng uppon bases abought the ponds in the pond yard — Payd to Heny Blankston of London, paynter, for paynting of 180 postes with white and greene in oyle and every poste conteyning 2½ yards deyppe at 16d. the yard standing in the kynge's new Garden, £32 : 6 : 8.

" Also for lyke paynting 96 pouncheons with white and greene and in oyle wrought with fine antyke upon both sydes, berying up the rayles in the said garden, £4 : 16 : 10.

" Also for paynting 960 yards in length of rayle.

" Kynges Beasts at the mount—Also payd Mych. of Hayles, kerver, for couttyng, makyng and karvyng of 16 of the kynges and the queenys beestes in tymber standyng about the mounte in the kynges new garden, the kynge finding stuff thereto at 20s. the pece, by convencyon, £16 : 0 : 0.

"Dials—To Bryce Augustine of Westmynster cloke-maker for making 16 brazin dials serving for the kynge's new garden at 4s. 4d. the piece.

"Trees—200 young treys of oake and elme—appul trees and pere trees—5 servys trees, 4 holly trees, quycksettes of woodbyne and thorne—treys of you—sypers, Genaper, and Bayes at 2d. the pece, 600 chery trees at 6d. the 100 —200 rose at 4d. the hundred, violettes, primroses, gitliver slips, mynts and other sweet flowers, sweet williams at 3d. the bushel—a bourder of rosemary 3 years old to set about the mount."

The actual posts and rails mentioned above are perhaps shown in the view of Hampton Court garden, which forms part of the back-ground to the contemporary picture of Henry VIII. and his family at Hampton Court.[1] Some idea of the size can be formed from the 960 yards of railing. The only fragment of Henry VIII.'s garden at Hampton Court is probably the small sunk garden close to the vine-house called the Pond garden. Soon after 1539 the great Palace of Nonsuch, near Cheam, in Surrey, was begun for Henry VIII. It is certain that Italian workmen were largely employed on this building ; and it is evident, from the description left by Hentzner, that

[1] Mr. Law, *History of Hampton Court Palace*, refers to a drawing by Wynegaarde in the Bodleian Library, and there is a remarkable view of these gardens in Tudor times in a picture of Queen Elizabeth, which was shown at the Tudor Exhibition. No. 310 — The plots are shown divided by sanded paths with wooden balustrades and terminals at the angles, not unlike the views in the *Hortus Floridus* of Crispin de Pass.— All the woodwork is painted red in the picture.

Italian examples were freely copied in this garden.[1] The kitchen garden and the fruit garden were separated, and the latter was surrounded by a wall 14 feet high, covered with rosemary. Hentzner noticed this practice of covering the whole surface of a wall with rosemary at Hampton Court and other places in England. " In the artificial pleasure gardens," he writes, " there are many columns and pyramids of marble, and two fountains of springing water — one shaped like a round, the other like a pyramid ; little birds spouting forth water sit on them. In the grove of Diana, in which is an artificial fountain, very pleasant to look upon, Actæon is being changed into a stag by the sprinkling of the goddess, with inscriptions underneath." Devices of this description, water-engines and elaborate hydraulic machines, were common in the great gardens of the sixteenth century. Hentzner mentions a curious sun-dial and fountain in the gardens at Whitehall which drenched the spectators if they came too close. Classical names and allusions were freely applied to the different parts of the garden. The garden at Theobalds, begun for Lord Burleigh in 1560, contained at one end a small mound called " the Mount of Venus." Hentzner gives a detailed account of this garden.

---

[1] Hentzner was a German who travelled through England in the sixteenth century and published an account of his travels in Latin at Nuremburg in 1598.

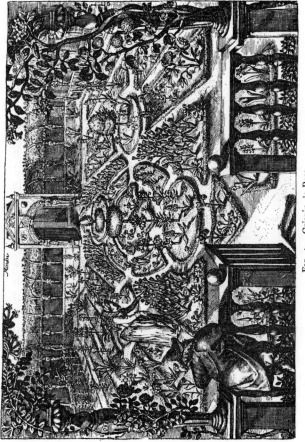

Fig. 4.—Crispin de Pass.

" Close to the palace is a garden surrounded on
all sides by water, so that any one in a boat may
wander to and fro among the fruit-groves with
great pleasure to himself.   There you will find
various trees and herbs, labyrinths made with
great pains, a fountain of springing water, of
white marble ; columns, too, and pyramids
placed about the garden—some of wood, some
of stone.   We were afterwards taken to the
garden-house by the gardener, and saw in the
ground floor, which is circular in shape, twelve
figures of Roman emperors in white marble,
and a table of Lydian stone.   The sides of the
upper floor are surrounded by lead tanks, into
which water is brought by pipes, so that fish
can be kept in them, and in summer-time one
can wash there in cold water.   In a banqueting-
room close to this room, and joined to it by a little
bridge, there was an oval table of red marble."
In an account written by Frederick, Duke of
Würzburg, in 1592, this table is described as of
black touchstone 14 spans long, 7 spans wide, and
1 span thick.   Peck, in his *Desiderata Curiosa*,
says of these gardens, "One might walk two myle
in the walkes before he came to their ends."

Gardens such as these were plainly inspired
by Italian examples,[1] and the Italian Renaissance garden was a close copy of the description

[1] Here again a distinction must be drawn between the earlier Italian
garden, such as that described in the text, and the later examples, such
as those of the Villa d'Este.

left by the post-Augustan writers, and more particularly by Pliny the younger. Pliny's account of his Tuscan villa abounds in architectural details, such as garden-houses adorned with marble and painting, fish-ponds and fountains in marble, and marble seats ; and Pliny, in describing the general lie of his house and grounds, uses the words *amoenitas tectorum*—a phrase curiously suggestive of the sweet, low lines of an Elizabethan manor-house. Clipped work, chiefly in box, is often mentioned in this account. The xystus, a space in front of the garden portico, was spaced out with box-trees, cut to various shapes, while the ground between was covered with figures of animals, set out flat on the ground, in clipped box. The paths were marked out with box edgings, and the intervening plots were filled either with grass or with box, cut into various devices, and sometimes in letters giving the name of the master or of the designer. In some of the paths stood obelisks, in others apple-trees, arranged alternately.[1] The resemblance between these details and a sixteenth-century garden is close, and it is to this source that we should look for the origin of shaped or cut work. The *topiarius*, or pleacher, was a very important person in the Roman garden, and the practice of cutting trees into various shapes was

[1] " Viae plures intercedentibus buxis dividuntur, alibi pratulum, alibi ipsa buxus intervenit, in formas mille descripta, literis interdum, quae modo nomen domini dicunt, modo artificis, alternis metulae surgunt alternis inserta sunt poma."—*Epistolae*, v. 6.

revived by the Italians of the fifteenth century.
The beautiful woodcuts to the *Hypneroto-
machia Poliphili* (Aldus, 1499) show several
designs of cut work.   Poliphilus dreams that he
and Pollia are conducted over the island of
Cythera ; and some curious illustrations are
given of the clipped box-trees in the enchanted
garden.   An English version of this book
appeared in England in 1592 ; but by this time
the habit of cutting box and yew and juniper
into different shapes was well established in
England.   Bacon refers to it in his well-known
Essay on Gardens, and the intricate hedge which
was to surround his main garden implies clipping on a most elaborate scale.   There is a
curious contemporary account of the garden
of Kenilworth in a letter from one of the
officers of the Court to Master Humphry
Martin, mercer, of London.   This letter was
written from Kenilworth in 1575, during
Elizabeth's visit to the castle.   In front of the
castle was a terrace walk raised 10 feet above
the garden, and 12 feet wide ; at either end
were arbours, " redolent by sweet trees and
flowers," and along the balustrade, on the garden
side, obelisks, spheres, and coats of arms in
stone were set out at equal distances.   Below
this terrace was the garden, an acre or more
in extent, divided into four quarters by fine
sanded walks.   In the centre of each plot rose
an obelisk of red porphyry with a ball at the

top. The garden was planted with apple-trees, pears, and cherries. In the middle of the wall opposite the terrace was a great aviary 30 feet long, 14 broad, and 20 high ; and in the centre of the garden a fountain of white marble rose out of an octagonal basin, "wherein pleasantly playing to and fro (were) carp, tench, bream, and for varietee pearch and eel—a garden then so appointed, as whearin aloft upon sweet shadowed walks of terras, in heat of soomer, to feel the pleasaunt whisking wynde above, or delectable coolness of the fountain spring beneath, to taste of delicious strawberries, cherris, and other fruites even from their stalks."

Bacon's garden, which should be taken in immediate connection with the palace of the preceding essay, was to be divided into three parts—a green, with a straight path across the centre, and covered walks at the sides ; then came the main garden, surrounded by an open arcade, with carpenter's work, with an "entire hedge of some 4 feet high above it," ornamented with little turrets and figures. In the centre of this garden was to be a mound, 30 feet high, and there was to be a banqueting-house, and fountains and tanks "finely paved," surrounded with images, and "embellished with coloured glasse and such things of lustre." Beyond this was to be "the heath" or wilderness, as it was afterwards called, a thicket of sweet-briar and honeysuckle, "and the ground set with violets, strawberries, primroses, and the like low flowers, being withal sweet and sightly." The English garden became in the sixteenth century a much more important affair in every way than it ever had been before ; much money was spent on it, and great care given to its design. Bacon talks of 30 acres of ground as the minimum for a prince's garden. But, apart from this matter of size and elaboration, the only specific importations from Italy appear to have been the use of terraces and balustrades and great flights of stairs, and the free use of statuary ; a habit of mythological allusion in various parts of the garden ; and the practice of clipping trees into various shapes, and distributing them symmetrically. The alleys, green walks, and covered walks, the "deambulationes ligneae horti," the arbours, the knots or figures, labyrinths and mazes, the conduits, tanks, and fountains, and particularly, the enclosing walls and definite boundary lines, were only the development of features which had existed already in the mediæval garden. Some of the more extravagant fancies which were caught up in England in the first flush of the Renaissance were abandoned in the following century. One doubts if any "little Figures with broad plates of round coloured glasse gilt for the sunne to play upon," perched on the top of a high hedge, were ever used in the seventeenth century. Caprices of this sort obtained no permanent

hold in England—the national tradition was too
sober to accept them—for in Bacon's own words
they were "nothing to the true pleasure of a
garden." And, again, it must be remembered
that Bacon's essay can no more be taken as an
accurate picture of the average garden of his
time than his *Essay on Building* as a representa-
tion of an ordinary Elizabethan house. Both
essays are ideal sketches, and Bacon's treatment
is purely literary ; with all its wealth of detail
it is exceedingly difficult to work out any
possible plan to fit the description given. The
gardens at Moor Park, told of by Sir William
Temple, were said to have been laid out on the
lines of this essay—probably the designer was
not careful to inform his client how much was
due to Bacon, and how much to the designer—
for when all is said, Bacon's ideas of design were
those of the amateur. Gardens appealed to him
only as so much literary material, and he wrote
a very charming essay on the subject, knowing
probably no more about it than any other
gentleman of his time. His most elaborate
treatise, the *Sylva Sylvarum*, deals with experiments and observations in horticulture, treated
as one application of his system of philosophy ;
but the book has no relation to garden design
at all.

Bacon, moreover, was not the first in the field
with his *Essay on Gardens*. Borde and Thomas
Hill had both dealt with the subject many years

earlier. Dr. Andrew Borde was an eccentric person of good education and abilities who was born in the latter part of the fifteenth century, and died in the Fleet in 1549. In the second chapter of a curious little book entitled the *Boke for to lerne a man to be wyse in buyldyng of his house for the health of his body, e to holde quyetnes for the helth of his soule and body*, etc., Borde discusses the question of "aspecte" and "prospecte." "My con-ceyte," he says, "is such, that I had rather not to buylde a mansyon or a house than to buylde one without a good prospect i to it i from it." The chief prospect is to be east, especially north-east, for the "est wynde·is temperat, fryske, and fragrant." This remarkable character of the east wind is repeated by Hill, and was, as Markham pointed out, the result of borrowing wholesale from Italian writers, without either acknowledging the source or correcting their statements by local experience. "Furthermore," says Borde, "it is a commodious and a pleasant thing in a mansyon to have an orcharde of sundrye fruytes, but it is more comodyous to have a fayre garden repleatyd with herbes of aromatyke and redolent savoures ; in the garden may be a poole or two for fysshe, yf the pooles be clene kept, also a park re-pleatyd with dere and conys is a necessary and a pleasant thynge " ; and the country gentle-man's residence is not complete without a " dove-cote, a payre of buttes for archery, and

a bowling alley." Thomas Hill was a volu-
minous writer who drew his materials mainly
from Latin authors. In 1563 he published
*A most briefe and pleasaunt treatyse teachynge
how to dress, sowe, and set a garden, gathered
out of the principallest authors in this art.*
Hill refers to Pliny and Columella, and deals
with aspect, with the choice of site, the qualities
of the ground, fencing and enclosures ; and to
these are added some notes on the properties of
plants and herbs, maxims as to the times and
seasons to be observed in planting, and remarks
on the signs of the zodiac. The book is a small
octavo, printed in black letter, and Hill states
that the "lyke, hitherto, hath not been published
in the Englishe tungue." The first edition is
lost. In 1568 he published a third edition
under the title of *The proffitable Arte of
Gardening*, with additions, treatises on bees,
and "yeerly conjectures meet for husbandmen
to know." Five subsequent editions of this
book were published in the years 1574, 1579,
1586, 1593, 1608. Two woodcuts of designs
for mazes are given—one circular in a square,
the other square ; these were to be formed,
"with Issop and Thyme or Lavender Cotton
spike masserome " ; in each angle of the square
was to be planted a fine fruit-tree, and "in the
myddle of it a proper herber decked with Roses
or else some fayre tree of Rosemary or other
Fruite." The third edition also contains five

knots for thyme or hyssop.   In 1577 a
new book appeared, entitled *The Gardener's
Labyrinth*, containing "a discourse of the
gardener's life, etc., wherein are set forth divers
Herbers, knots, and mazes, cunningly handled
for the beautifying of gardens, etc., gathered

FIG. 5.—From *The Gardener's Labyrinth*.

out of the best approved writers of Garden-
ing, Husbandrie, and Physicke, by Didymus
Mountaine."   It appears, from the dedication
to Lord Burghley, that this book was edited by
Henry Dethicke after the death of Mountaine.
The book is nothing more than an enlarged
edition of Thomas Hill's *Profitable Art*.
Much of the text and several of the woodcuts

Fig. 6.—From *The Gardener's Labyrinth.*

are reproduced exactly, and it would seem almost certain that "Didymus Mountaine" is no other than Thomas Hill, and that Master Dethicke yielded to the temptation to exploit materials collected by another man. Dethicke or "Mountaine" leads off with a grand list of twenty-eight authors, in which "Vergile" appears between Palladius Rutilius and Didymus, and Hesiod stands next to Africanus. The first part deals with the garden, the second with the distillation of herbs. Some suggestions are given for the formation of arbours and labyrinths and the spacing of beds and alleys, but the greater part of the book is taken up with advice as to planting, and quotations from authors, such as "the skilful Rutilius," "the learned Democritus," "the worthie Pliny," and "the well-practised Apuleius." Generally speaking, the writer conceived of a garden as a small enclosed space, with a broad walk inside the wall on all four sides of a rectangular plot; and the latter was to be subdivided into a number of smaller plots divided by narrow alleys. The maze, or the labyrinth, or any of the various knots, would occupy one of the smaller plots. The book is written in a tedious style, and with much repetition. Its value consists in the light which it throws on the average English garden of the sixteenth century, as contrasted with the princely garden sketched by Bacon. A further point of interest in the book is its curious superstition. The gardener is carefully to observe the moon and the aspect of the planets before he sows. Thus " the moone increasing and running between the 28 degree of Taurus and the xi degree of the signe Gemini, sow fine seedes, and plant daintie herbes ; but the moone found between the 28th degree of Gemini and the exit of Cancer (although she increase) yet bestow no daintie seeds in your earth." As a protection against hail, Mountaine suggests a device of Philostratus. You drag a "Marsh tortoise " round the garden on its back, and then place it still on its back on a little mound, carefully banking it up, so that the tortoise cannot tumble over or do anything but flap its legs. This is supposed to frighten away the hail. Thomas Hill mentions that a " speckled toad, enclosed in an earthen pot " was considered another good remedy.

Hill, like Bacon, was not a designer, or even a practical fruit-grower. Bacon wrote as a literary man, and Hill as a compiler of manuals. The first attempt to deal with the laying out of gardens in the light of actual experience was made by Gervase Markham, who set himself to write a complete account of the knowledge and accomplishments which became the country gentleman. Markham is English of the English, and the most delightful of writers. He had an amazing contempt for his pre-decessors, who, in writing on gardens, had

contented themselves with quoting from Latin
and Italian writers, "whence it comes that our
Englishe book knowledge in these cases is both
disgraced and condemned, every one fayling in
his experiments, because he is guided by no
home-bred but a stranger, as if to read the
Englishe tongue there were none better than
an Italian pedant" (*The English Husbandman*).
"Contrary to all other authors, I am neither
beholding to Pliny, Virgil, Columella, etc. . . .
according to the plaine true Englishe fashion,
thus I pursue my purpose." As a matter of
fact, his first treatise, *The Country Farm*,
1615, consisted mainly of translations from the
French of Olivier de Serres. In regard to
general arrangement of house and grounds,
Markham gives a plan evidently based on the
yeoman's house, such as is found in the Weald
of Kent. The house was to be placed north and
south. In front there was to be a small fore
court enclosed with a fence, which might be
replaced by a gate-house or terrace; at the
back of the house was the base court, with a
"faire large pond well stoned and gravelled in
the bottom," in the centre. On the north side
of the base court were the stables, cow-houses,
and swine-cotes; on the south side, the barns and
poultry-houses; on the west side, joining these
two arms, the lodges, with cart-shed under. The
garden was to be on the south side of the house.
Markham gives separate rules for the garden

and the orchard, but they were practically laid
out on the same lines. He further separates
the kitchen garden from the garden of pleasure,
and subdivides the latter into two parts : (1)
The nosegay garden, to be planted with violets,
gillyflowers, marigolds, lilies and daffodils, and
" such strange flowers as hyacinths, dulippos,
narcissus, and the like " ; (2) the garden of
herbs, set with southern-wood, rosemary, hyssop,
lavender, basil, rue, tansy, all-good, marierome,
pennyroyal, and mint. The garden, like the
orchard, might either be laid out as a single
square, subdivided by cross paths into four
quarters, or as a series of squares, two, or three,
or more, on different levels. In the latter case
each square was to be raised 8 feet or so (he
also says seven or eight steps) above the lower
level, and to be reached by " convenient staires
of state " ; over this ascent " there might be
built some curious and artificiall banqueting-
house." A broad path would run round each
square, with paths of the same width forming
the four quarters, and in the centre might be
placed " either a conduit of some anticke
fashion, a standard of some unusuall devise,
or else some Dyall or other Pyramid thet may
grace and beautifie the garden." Both garden
and orchard were to be surrounded with a
stone or brick wall, if possible, or failing that,
" a high strong pale, or a great ditch with quick-
set hedge." All the quarters to the squares

FIG. 7.—Knots from Markham's *Country Farm.*

should be planted differently, and a series of knots or interlacing figures are given, which were to be planted with germander, hyssop, thyme, pink gillyflowers, or thrift, with borders of lavender, rosemary, or box. The noticeable point in Markham's account of the gardens is the emphasis with which he insists on the necessity of ordered design, not only for all kinds of gardens, but for the orchards and fish-ponds as well. Everything is to be laid out in comely order. The kitchen garden is not to be a dreary wilderness of vegetables, but should have its broad trim paths, its borders of lavender or roses, its well or fountain, and even its arbours or "turrets of lattice fashion," as in the garden of pleasure. One finds no sugges-tion in Markham of "improving nature"; the point would never have occurred to him whether nature was to be improved or dis-improved; but, on the other hand, one does find in him a genuine love of nature, of the music of birds, of the sweet scent of flowers and all their dainty colouring. His influence through the seventeenth century was con-siderable; several of his treatises were published in a collected form under the title of *A Way to get Wealth*, and this book went through fifteen editions, the last appearing as late as 1695, when the school of Le Nôtre was well in the ascendant.

William Lawson was a friend of Markham's,

and wrote, like the latter, out of his own experience. In 1618 he published *A New Orchard and Garden*, being, as he says in the title-page, "the labours of forty-eight years, more particularly in Yorkshire." Lawson seems to have lived in Holdernesse. An orchard with Lawson meant, in the strictest sense, an apple garden, for it was to be laid out with large walks, broad and long, having seats of camomile, and enclosed with walls or moats, and to have borders and beds of sweet flowers, and cut work in "lesser wood," mazes, and bowling alleys, and a pair of butts; and "one chief grace that adornes an orchard, I cannot let slippe; a brood of nightingales, who with their several notes and tunes, with a strong delightsome voyce out of a weake body, will bear you company night and day . . . the gentle robbin red-breast will helpe her, . . . neither will the silly wren be behind in Summer, with her distinct whistle (like a sweet Recorder) to cheere your spirits." Lawson lays it down as a matter of course that a garden should be square, and gives some designs for knots for the square beds in *The Countrie Housewife's Garden*, 1617. The kitchen garden and flower garden should be divided, but you are not to neglect beauty in the kitchen garden, and you may therefore make "comely borders to the beds, with Roses, Lavender, and the like." The most delightful chapter in *The New Orchard* is that

FIG. 8.—From Lawson's *New Orchard.*

A. All these squares must be set with trees; the gardens and other ornaments must stand in spaces betwixt the trees and in the borders and fences.

B. Trees 20 yards asunder.

C. Garden knot.

D. Kitchen garden. | E. Bridge.

F. Conduit. | G. Staires.

H. Walkes set with great wood thicke.

I. Walkes set with great wood round about your orchard.

K. The out-fence.

L. The out-fence set with stone fruit.

M. Mount. To force earth for a mount or such like, set it round with quick, and lay boughs of trees strangely intermingled, tops inward, with the earth in the middle.

N. Still-house.

O. Good standing for bees if you have an house.

P. If the river run by your doore and under your mount it will be pleasant.

which deals with the ornaments of the garden.
The words seem instinct with the sweetness
and simplicity of the old-world garden.   Lawson
is a writer for whom one forms a personal
affection.   He is less precise and business-like
than Bacon, who wrote of these things as an
accomplished man of the world ; Lawson is
altogether more sincere and unworldly, his
humour is gentler, his style more gracious and
musical, and he wrote with a sense of what is
beautiful in nature which could only come from
long musings among the flowers and many a
leisurely hour in the trim alleys of his garden.
Of a sense so delicate as this, Bacon was incap-
able.   "What can your eye desire to see, your
eare to heare, your mouth to taste, or your
nose to smell that is not to be had in an
orchard with abundance and beauty?   What
more delightsome than an infinite varietie of
sweet smelling flowers ? decking with sundrye
colours the greene mantle of the earth, the
universal mother of us all, so by them bespotted,
so dyed, that all the world cannot sample them,
and wherein it is more fit to admire the Dyer
than imitate his workmanship, colouring not
only the earth but decking the ayre, and
sweetening every breath and spirit.

   "The rose red, damaske, velvet, and double
double province rose, the sweet muske rose
double and single, the double and single white
rose, the faire and sweet scenting woodbind

double and single ; Purple cowslips and double cowslips, primrose double and single, the violet nothing behind the best for smelling sweetly, and a thousand more will provoke your contente, and all these by the skill of your Gardener so comely and orderly placed in your Borders and squares."

Lawson's work is typical of the most charming side of the Renaissance in England, of its delight in flowers and birds, and all rare and beautiful things in art and nature ; but Bacon's weight of intellect bore down this subtle delicate instinct, and the treatises on this subject for the next fifty years follow the lines of *The Sylva Sylvarum* rather than *The New Orchard and Garden.*

CHAPTER III

THE FORMAL GARDEN—*continued*

IT has been usual in dealing with gardens to include some account of the numerous Herbals which were published in England in the sixteenth and seventeenth centuries. Strictly speaking, these lie outside the scope of my subject ; the Herbals are little more than *catalogues raisonnés* of the various fruits and flowers grown in England at the time, with notes on their medicinal qualities, and instructions as to the proper times and methods of planting. This has nothing to do with garden design. As, however, the distinction between garden design, horticulture, and botany was never very clearly made, I give the dates of the principal Herbals.

Mr. Hazlitt gives a complete list of the bibliography of gardening, but, as will appear from the titles of the works there mentioned, for the next fifty years after Lawson's book, nearly all the treatises which are not Herbals deal with horticulture. *The Great Herbal*, from the French, was first published in 1516 ; *The Little Herbal*, from the Latin, in 1525. Cary's *Book of the Properties of Herbs*, and Macer's *Herbal* were published about 1540 ; Ascham's *Little Herbal*, 1550 ; Turner's *Herbal*, 1551 to 1568 ; Lyte's translation of Dodoens's *Herbal*, 1578 ; John Gerard's *Herbal* in 1597 ; John Parkinson's well-known book, *Paradisi in Sole Paradisus Terrestris*, *The Garden of Pleasure*, was published in 1629. His Herbal or *Theatre of Plants* followed in 1640. Gerard had a famous physic garden in Holborn, near Ely Place, overlooking the Fleet. This was one of the earliest of the botanical gardens which reached such a high pitch of perfection in the latter half of the seventeenth century, as, for instance, the well-known Botanical Garden at Oxford which was founded and presented to the University by the Earl of Danby in 1632. A botanical garden and museum was kept in South Lambeth by John Tradescant. Isaac Walton gives some particulars of the Tradescants. The grandfather and father were gardeners to Queen Elizabeth, the son to Charles I. The father and son travelled over Europe and the East in search of plants, and the son is said to have travelled in Virginia for the same purpose. His *Catalogue* was not published till 1662. The collection formed by the Tradescants was purchased by Mr. Ashmole, who gave it to

the University of Oxford, and it thus became
the basis of the Ashmolean collection.   In lists
of garden books of this period the name of
Sir Hugh Platt often occurs, and the titles of
his books, *The Garden of Eden* and *Flora's
Paradise* raise expectations which are uniformly
disappointed.   Platt says he will not trouble
his readers with rules for the shaping and
fashioning of an orchard—" every Drawer or
embroiderer, nay, almost each Dancing-master,
may pretend to such niceties," and having thus
demolished the necessity of such a poor thing
as the designer, Platt unfolds his own learning
in a meagre string of amateur notes on plants.
Platt was only a dabbler in science, and from
our point of view stands on a very different
footing from such men as Markham and Lawson.
Both of the latter were thoroughly familiar with
the garden, not only as practical gardeners, but
as designers of gardens.   They do not appear
to have had any special training in design, but
they were evidently familiar with the accepted
methods of garden design, and there is an
important difference between the country gentleman of the seventeenth century and his successor
in the nineteenth.   The latter has little traditional knowledge of design, and the arts of
design form no part of his education, whereas
the English gentleman from the sixteenth to
the eighteenth century did possess a general
traditional knowledge of design and of the

principles which govern it. He was not better educated, but he succeeded to an excellent way of doing things as the result of many generations of experience and uninterrupted development, instead of having to choose between half a dozen different ways, with all of which he is equally unfamiliar. It was thus that, in the seventeenth century, the country gentleman might be able to lay out his own garden, because, with trifling variations, he laid it out on the same lines as his father and his grandfather before him.

In more important work, however, there seems little doubt that the architect, or rather the architect builder, as he usually was, designed the grounds as well as the house, and this continued to be the custom till the days of Capability Brown. Du Cerceau, in the plates of his *Les Plus Excellents Bastiments*, gives quite as much attention to the gardens as to the palaces ; and in all books of illustration throughout the seventeenth century, house and grounds are shown as a whole. There is a small plan of a house and garden by John Thorpe in the Soane Museum, which shows a square house, with courts in back and front, and garden at the side, divided into four main plots, subdivided into smaller knots and squares. On the back court is written a note " nothing out of square." John Thorpe died early in the seventeenth century. The distinction of all these earlier seventeenth-century garden plans is the extreme simplicity of their arrangement. However rich the details, there is no difficulty in grasping the principle of a garden laid out in an equal number of rectangular plots. Everything is straightforward and logical ; you are not bored with hopeless attempts to master the bearings of the garden. The old gardens at Wilton, designed by Isaac de Caux, were laid out in three divisions, each divided into two by a broad path running down the centre, with cross paths running to the outer walks. Isaac de Caux, or Caus, was a German architect, resident in England in the early part of the seventeenth century, and in the employment of the Court. He laid out the gardens at Wilton for the Earl of Pembroke, and published a series of twenty-six copper-plates to illustrate these gardens in detail, with the following description :—

"This Garden, within the enclosure of the new wall is a thowsand foote long and about Foure hundred in breadthe divided in its length into three long squares or parallelograms, the first of which divisions next the building, heth ffoure Platts, embroydered ; in the midst of which are ffoure fountaynes with statues of marble in their midle, and on the sides of those Platts are the Platts of fflowers, and beyond them is the little Terrass rased for the more advantage of beholding those Platts, this for the first division.   In the second are two Groves or woods all with divers walkes, and through those Groves passeth the river Nader having of breadth in this place 44 foote upon which is built the bridge of the breadth of the greate walke.   In

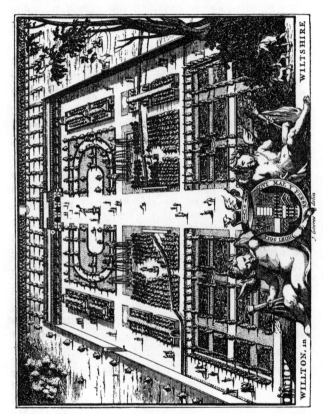

Fig. 9.—Wilton, from De Caux.

the midst of the aforesayd Groves are two great statues of
white marble, of eight ffoote high, the one of Bacchus and
the other Flora, and on the sides ranging with the Platts
of fflowers are two covered Arbors of 300 ffoote long and
diverse allies.   Att the beginning of thee third and last
division, are on either side of the great walke, two Ponds
with Fountaynes and two Collumnes in the midle, casting
water all their height which causeth the moveing and
turning of two crownes att the top of the same and beyond
is a Compartment of greene with diverse walkes planted
with Cherrie trees and in the midle is the Great oval with
the Gladiator of brass ; the most famous Statue of all that
antiquity hath left.   On the sydes of this compartiment
and answering the Platts of flowers and long arbours are
three arbours of either side with twining Galleryes
communicating themselves one into another.   Att the end
of the greate walke is a Portico of stone cutt and adorned
with Pilasters and Nyches within which are 4 ffigures of
white marble of 5 ffoote high.   On either side of the sayd
portico is an assent leading up to the terrasse upon the
steps whereof instead of Ballasters are sea monsters casting
water from one and the other from the top to the bottome,
and above the sayd portico is a great reserve of water for
the grotto.''

De Caux was superseded, both at Court and
in the employment of the Earl of Pembroke, by
Inigo Jones.   James I. had a French gardener
in his employment named André Mollet, who
came of a family of famous garden designers.
His father was said to have invented the
jardin brodé, and wrote a book entitled *Le
Théâtre des Plantes et Jardinages*, for which
André Mollet supplied designs.   These and
other designs by Mollet were published at
Stockholm in 1651, as *Le Jardin de Plaisir*,

*contintant plusieurs dessins de jardinage, tant
parterres en Broderie, compartiments de gazon,
que Bosquets et autres.* On the title-page of
this book Mollet is described as " Maistre des
Jardins de la sérénissime Reine de Suède."

The period from the outbreak of the Civil
War to the Restoration is, comparatively speaking, a blank in the history of the arts. Evelyn
records the destruction of part of the gardens
at Nonsuch by the Puritans ; writing in 1666,
he says : " There stand in the garden two
handsome stone pyramids, and the avenue
planted with rowes of faire elmes ; but the rest
of these goodly trees both of this and Worcester
Park adjoyning, were felled by those destructive
& avaricious rebels in the late war, which
defaced one of the stateliest seats his Majesty
had." No one did more than Evelyn to
encourage the study of horticulture in England ;
he wrote treatises and translations[1] himself, and
induced Worlidge and others to write on the
subject ; but though fully alive to the beauty of
a well-designed garden, he paid less attention
to the question of garden design, foreseeing,
perhaps, the chaos which was to follow the interference of the man of letters in the eighteenth
century. It seems that Evelyn did contemplate a
book on garden design, under the title of *Elysium*

[1] *The English Vineyard*, 1663 ; *Sylva*, 1664 ; *Kalendarium Hortense*,
1666 ; *The French Gardiner*, translated by J. E., 1672 ; *Of Gardens*, by
Rapin, translated by J. E., 1673 ; *The Compleat Gardener*, De la Quintinye,
translated 1693 ; *Directions concerning Melons*, 1693.

Britannicum. This work would have been a most exhaustive treatise. It was to have consisted of three books—the first dealing with the soil of the garden and the seasons, the second with garden design under twenty-one heads, the third with the means of producing rare species, distilling, and various miscellaneous points. I give in an appendix a complete list of the subdivisions. Unfortunately Evelyn never carried out his intention ; but the titles left by him are important, as showing how Evelyn conceived of a garden, and the clear distinction which existed in his mind between garden design and horticulture.

With the Restoration a change came over the designs of the larger English gardens. Charles II. was in intimate relations with the brilliant Court of Louis XIV., at a time when the latter was in the full swing of his magnificence, and when architects such as Mansard and Perrault were seconded by a designer of such remarkable genius as Le Nôtre. The noble paths and terraces, the great avenues and masses of foliage, the broad expanse of grass and water in which Le Nôtre delighted, became the fashion in England. Whatever faults Le Nôtre may have had (and to the landscapist he represents all that is detestable), he was at least a man of large ideas and scholarly execution. He carried the art of garden design to the highest point of develop-

ment it has ever reached, and this by no
violent reform or blundering originality, but
by profound thought on the lines laid down by
his predecessors. Something of the grandeur
of Le Nôtre, some flavour of his lordly
manner, spread to England, and for the next
fifty years or so the grounds of the great
noblemen's country-houses were laid out on a
scale compared with which even Bacon's 30
acres seems a trifling affair ; for Le Nôtre
had covered 200 acres with gardens at Versailles, and the great terrace which he built
at St. Germain-en-Laye is 1½ mile long and
115 feet wide.   There is a story that Le
Nôtre actually came to England to lay out the
grounds of Greenwich and St. James's Parks ;
but there appears to be no evidence of this.
There is a plan of the palace and grounds of
St. James's in Kip's book. The gardens covered
the whole of the space now taken up by
Marlborough House and Carlton House Terrace,
and terminated in a grove laid out as a *patte-
d'oie*, or goose foot, on the site now occupied
by the offices of the London County Council
and other buildings.   A straight canal bordered
by double rows of trees extended from the
Chelsea Gate to opposite the Tiltyard. The
only vestige of the original laying out is the
quadruple avenue which runs from Buckingham
Palace to Spring Gardens. It is also doubtful
whether Le Nôtre personally had anything to

do with Hampton Court, but it is plain that the general arrangement of the grounds in front of Wren's Buildings was due to his influence, and it is known that the great *Fountain Garden* was first laid out for Charles II. The enormous semicircle, with the three radiating avenues and the great centre canal, the intricate *parterres de broderie*, shown in Kip's view, and above all, the masterly conception of the grounds as a whole and in strict relation to the architecture of the palace, were certainly inspired by the influence of Le Nôtre, if not actually due to his design. There is no mention or any indication of the use of avenues on this scale before the Restoration. Indeed, Worlidge, whose book was published in 1677, specifically says : "It was not long since our choicest avenues were first planted with those ornamental shades that now are become common." There is therefore good reason for assigning the origin of this feature to French influence. Individual avenues were, of course, in use before this date. Switzer says : "About the reign of Queen Elizabeth of immortal memory we may suppose some of the old avenues and walks adjoining noblemen's houses were planted." These, however, should be distinguished from the system of avenues radiating from one centre which was now introduced from France.

The landscape gardener of the following

century, and his far less able followers in this, have had ideas of modifying a landscape by planting trees here and there or in clumps, or by throwing out woods, or by many more of their favourite devices for " chastening nature's graceful touch " ; but their ideas are paltry when contrasted with the comprehensive scale on which designers went to work after the Restoration. The main avenue at Bushey Park, 1 mile long and 60 feet wide, with a row of chestnuts next the road, and four rows of limes on either side, with the great "Diana" basin at Hampton Court, 400 feet diameter, was carried out by Wise in 1699 at a cost of £4300. Very few of these gigantic schemes remain intact, though there is a notable instance on the Boughton estate, near Kettering, where one suddenly finds one's self in the presence of avenues miles away from the house to which they relate. Part of the original laying out of the grounds of Wrest in Bedfordshire remains, and there are, of course, many instances of isolated avenues. Fortunately, however, four publishers—Mortier, Midwinter, Overton, and Smith—took it into their heads to publish a series of elaborate double plates in folio, illustrating the great country seats of England at the end of the seventeenth century, under the title of *Britannia Illustrata*. The drawings for this series were made by a man named Knyff,[1] of

---

[1] Knyff was a painter of dogs and poultry, who died in 1721 ; Jan

whom little is known, and were engraved on copper by John Kip. The book was published in 1709, though many of the drawings were made much earlier, and is absolutely invaluable for a knowledge of the method of laying out gardens and grounds on a large scale at the end of the seventeenth century. Kip's book, Bade-slade's *Views of Kent* (1772), and another book named *Les Délices de la Grande Bretagne*, are in fact almost the only sources of information available, as very few of these great schemes remain intact. The park and gardens at Badminton are a typical instance. Kip gives three views of Badminton—the illustration in the text is taken from the smaller print in *Les Délices*, 1727. The approach to the house was formed by a triple avenue, the centre avenue 200 feet wide, the two side avenues 80 feet wide. The entrance gates to this avenue were placed in the centre of a great semicircular wall. The distance from this gateway to the house was $2\frac{1}{2}$ miles. After passing through two more gateways, the avenue opened on to a great oblong open space forming part of the deer park, with avenues on either side, and the entrance gate to the fore court of the house opposite the end of the main avenue. A broad gravelled path, with grass plots and fountains on either side, led from the

Kip was born in Amsterdam in 1652. He came to England soon after the Restoration, and engraved views for Atkyns's *Gloucester Survey*, and Badeslade's *Views of Kent*. He died in 1722.

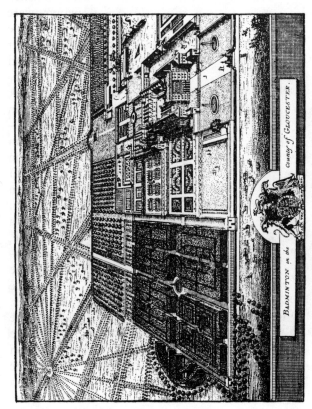

BADMINTON in the county of GLOUCESTER.

Fig. 10.—Badminton, from *Les Délices de la Grande Bretagne*.

entrance gate of the fore court to a flight of
four steps leading to the pavement in front of
the house.   Kip's view shows a coach and six
approaching the entrance gate, apparently not
on the road but on the grass of the park.   To
the right hand was the base court, with stables
and outhouses ; at the back of the house the
kitchen and fruit gardens and the pigeon-house.
To the left of the house and fore court were
the bowling-green and pleasure gardens, with
the grove beyond.   The latter was divided into
four plots, with four-way paths and a circular
space and fountain in the centre.   Each of the
plots was planted with close-growing trees laid
out as mazes, and trimmed close and square for
a height apparently of some 15 to 20 feet from
the ground.   Opposite the centre alley was a
semicircular bay divided into quadrants, each
quadrant with a basin and fountain and great
square hedges trimmed to the same height as
the rest of the grove.   The whole of these
immense gardens were walled in, with the exception of a fence round the grove.   Wide
gates were set at the ends of all the main paths,
and from these, as points of departure, avenues
were laid out in straight lines, radiating and
intersecting each other in all directions.   If
Kip's figures are correct, some of these avenues,
which extended beyond the park to the villages
in the adjacent country, were 6 or 7 miles long.
As shown on plans these avenues look bizarre

and unattractive, but in actual fact—that is, when the trees are fully grown—their effect is very fine. And here, again, the straightforwardness, or what one might call the honesty of the formal method is clearly shown. If a landscape is to be altered, it may just as well be altered frankly ; and these designers, liking long lines of trees and the vistas of great avenues, planted their straight lines without any affectation that the work was nature's. At the same time this practice was, perhaps, the first sign of the coming decadence. It was a failure in that strictly logical system which separated the garden from the park, and left the latter to take care of itself—a system which frankly subordinated nature to art within the garden wall, but in return gave nature an absolutely free hand outside it. These avenues and rides were an attempt to manipulate the face of an entire countryside, and gave a point of departure to the futilities of Brown and the improvers of nature in the following century.

Generally speaking, the influence of Le Nôtre and his school showed itself in the increased scale of English gardens, and in greater elaboration of detail. The gardens of Melbourne Hall, in Derbyshire, are a perfect instance of the French manner in England on a moderate scale. These gardens were remodelled and considerably enlarged for Thomas Coke, afterwards vice - chamberlain to George I., from

LEAD VASE : MELBOURNE : DERBYSHIRE :

Fig. 11.

designs by Henry Wise between 1704 and 1711.
The older garden appears to have consisted
of a terrace, with two levels below it and
red-brick walls on either side. The lower
wall was probably removed, and an extensive
bosquet or grove planted, with a great water-
piece and several smaller fountains. Long
alleys with palisades of limes were formed, and
an amphitheatre of limes, with vistas radiating
in all directions from a superb lead urn in the
centre. The ground is of irregular plan, but
the difficulties are met by the design in a most
masterly manner. Some alterations were made
in the garden about fifty years ago. Otherwise
the original design is substantially perfect, and
is a very valuable instance of a garden laid out
when the French influence was still dominant
in England. This influence, however, was
practically limited to the grounds of men of
large estate, and the gardens of the smaller gentry
were laid out on a much less costly scale,
and without any great departure from traditional lines. The gardens of Doddington, in
Lincolnshire, or Dunham Massie, in Cheshire,
as presented by Kip, show little or no French
influence ; and the small gardens shown in
Logan's views of the Colleges of Oxford
and Cambridge might have been laid out by
Gervase Markham or William Lawson himself. The Oxford and Cambridge gardens
most effectually meet the objection to the

formal style that it requires great space. Unfortunately, the original design has been destroyed in all these gardens, but their main dimensions have not been altered, and Logan's views give a very accurate idea of their general character.[1]

Meanwhile, there was a vigorous revival in the literature of gardens. Little or nothing had been written on the laying out of gardens since the time of Markham and Lawson. In 1665 appeared *Flora, Ceres, and Pomona,* by John Rea, Gent. The greater part of this book is taken up with descriptions of flowers, plants, and fruit-trees, and horticultural notes. But the introduction to the first book contains some account of the proper ordering of a "garden of delight,"—that is, of the Fruit garden and the Flower garden. Rea wrote his book in his old age, and after forty years' practice as a planter of gardens, and though he describes his work as a " Florilege " and an innovation on the old method of the Herbal, with a sly dig at

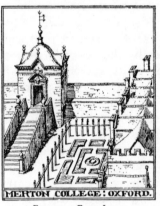

FIG. 12.—From Logan.

[1] Logan's *Oxonia Illustrata*, 1675 ; *Cantabrigia Illustrata*.

Mr. Parkinson by the way, he was a thorough-
going adherent of the old school of design.
He speaks with some contempt of "gardens of
the new model" laid out with good walks and
grass plots, and fountains, grottoes, statues, etc.,
but destitute of flowers, probably referring to
some bad applications of French ideas.   Rea
did Le Nôtre injustice in implying that his
method made no use of flowers ; Madame de
Sévigné, writing to her daughter in 1678, about
Le Nôtre's work at Clagny, says, " Vous
connaissez la manière de Le Nostre . . . ce
sont des allées où l'on est à l'ombre, et pour
cacher les caisses " (for the orange-trees) " il y a,
de deux côtés, des palissades, à hauteur d'appui,
toutes fleuries de tuberoses, de roses, de jasmins,
d'œillets ; c'est assurément la plus belle, la plus
surprenante et la plus enchantée nouveauté qui
se puisse imaginer." The garden which Rea
contemplated was, of course, walled in.   He
talks of 40 yards square as the proper size
for a private gentleman's fruit garden, and half
this size for his flower garden.   The flower
gardens were to be laid out in simple geometrical
patterns, for which he gives sixteen excellent
designs which show no trace at all of French
influence.   In 1670 appeared *The English
Gardener*, by Leonard Meager, the third part of
which deals with "the ordering of the garden
of pleasure, with variety of knots and wilderness work after the best fashion." He gives a

few diagrams of knots and designs for quarters, but says very little to the purpose on garden design.   In 1697 Meager published another book entitled *The New Art of Gardening*, but both his works are inferior in value to the *Systema Horticulturæ, or Art of Gardening*, by J. W., Gent., published in 1677, "illustrated with sculptures representing the form of gardens according to the newest models."   J. W. is John Worlidge.   His work consists of three books, and describes the details of the garden with some minuteness.   The shape of the garden, its general plan, its walls and fences, its walks and arbours, terraces, seats, pleasure-houses, fountains and water - works, statues, obelisks, and dials, are all successively dealt with, and followed by a systematic treatise on the flowers and trees with which the gardens should be planted.   Worlidge repeated Rea's complaint as to the banishment of flowers, and the excessive use of sculpture in gardens, but his garden was perfectly formal and did not depart from the traditional lines in any sense whatever.   No serious change was introduced under William and Mary, except that the habit of clipping yew and box trees was carried to an excess that made it an easy prey for the sarcasm of Pope in the following century.   The Dutch were fond of queer little trifles, and used to cut their trees into every conceivable shape. Switzer says that " this fashion was brought

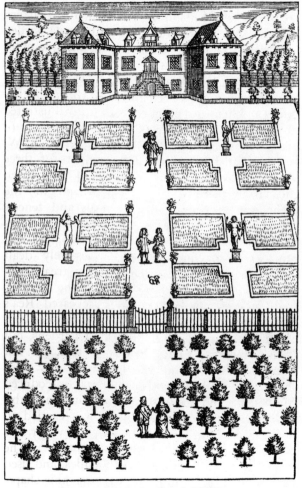

Fig. 13.—A Garden, from J. Worlidge.

over out of Holland by the Dutch gardeners, who used it to a fault, especially in England, where we abound in so good grass and gravel "; but Switzer is inaccurate here, for the custom of " pleaching " was an old one in England. It now, however, developed into a positive mania for cocks and hens and other conceits in yew and box, and for little clipped trees spaced symmetrically along the sides of the walks, as they are shown in nearly all Kip's views, and particularly in the views of Wimple and Staunton Harold. In the latter there is a suggestion of a whole menagerie in clipped work along the sides of the great basin. Peter Collinson notes that " the gardens about London in 1712 were remarkable for fine cut greens and clipt yews in the shape of birds, dogs, men, ships, etc." The curious cut work in the gardens of Levens Hall, in Westmoreland, is a well-known instance. This garden was planted early in the eighteenth century, and is evidently a deliberate copy of a Dutch model. The difference between the French influence and the Dutch is very well shown by the contrast between the gardens of Melbourne and Levens ; there is something a little childish about the latter. In the garden of Risley Hall, in Derbyshire, there is a charming instance of cut yew—two doves about 7 feet long billing each other form an archway in a yew hedge ; but the most remarkable instance still exists at Packwood, in Warwickshire, where

Fig. 14.

TOPIARY WORK AT LEVENS HALL : WESTMORELAND

the Sermon on the Mount is literally represented in clipped yew. At the entrance to the "mount," at the end of the garden, stand four tall yews 20 feet high for the four evangelists, and six on either side for the twelve apostles. At the top of the mount is an arbour formed in a great yew-tree called the "pinnacle of the temple," which was also supposed to represent Christ on the Mount overlooking the evangelists, apostles, and the multitude below; at least, this account of it was given by the gardener, who was pleaching the pinnacle of the temple.

RISLEY : DERBYSHIRE.

CHAPTER IV

THE END OF THE FORMAL GARDEN AND THE LANDSCAPE SCHOOL

When William and Mary began their reign gardening was already the fashionable hobby. Charles II. had patronised it in his casual manner : he began the great semicircle at Hampton Court and the gardens and park of St. James ; and for fifty years we find a succession of famous gardeners. Rose, who had studied under Le Nôtre, was gardener to Charles II. ; London was pupil to Rose, and Switzer pupil or servant to London and Wise. The great nursery at Brompton, which, in the following century, was estimated to contain plants to the value of £30,000 to £40,000, was founded by a company of these men—London, gardener to

Compton, Bishop of London, Cook to the Earl of Essex, Lucre to the Queen Dowager at Somerset House, Field to the Earl of Bedford. According to Switzer, this firm laid out the gardens at Longleat, each of the partners staying there one month in turn. Lucre and Field died, and London bought out Cook, and shortly afterwards took Wise into partnership. George London and Henry Wise were the two most celebrated English gardeners of their time. London was "superintendent of their Majesties' gardens" at £200 a year, and a page of the backstairs to Queen Mary. Besides the royal gardens, the firm directed most, of the great gardens of England. Hampton Court, Kensington Gardens, Blenheim, Wanstead, in Essex, Edger, in Herts, and Melbourne, in Derbyshire, were among their principal works. London seems to have fallen out of favour with Queen Anne. Switzer says, "Queen Anne (of pious memory) committed the care of her gardens in chief to Mr. Wise, Mr. London still pursuing his business in the country." London used to divide his business into circuits, spending six weeks on his northern circuit, and riding 50 to 60 miles a day; and it appears from a flaming advertisement, published by Evelyn at the beginning of his translation of De la Quintinye, that London and Wise undertook garden design of all sorts, as well as horticulture. Switzer, who had his own advertisement to make, speaks

J. Kip Delin. et Sculp.

Fig. 15.—From Atkyns's *Gloucestershire*.

in rather disparaging terms of London's power as a designer. Both London and Wise seem to have been taken by the Dutch manner, though London, at any rate, had seen the great French gardens, and in his design for the gardens of Melbourne, 1704, he was much more influenced by French than by Dutch examples. In 1706 London and Wise published *The Retired Gard'ner*, a translation from *Le Jardinier Solitaire*, and a treatise of the Sieur Louis

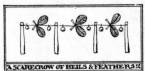

FIG. 16.—From London and Wise.

Liger of Auxerre, with corrections by the translators. The only substantial addition which London and Wise made to this book was a description of the garden laid out by them for Marshal Tallard [1] at Nottingham. London died in 1713. He lived just long enough to see all the boxwork at Hampton Court, which he had planted for William, pulled up by Queen Anne.

Another translation from the French appeared in 1712, entitled *The Theory and Practice of Gardening, done from the French Original, by John James of Greenwich*. It is not known who wrote the original. It has been attributed both to D'Argenville Dezalliers and to Le Blond, pupils of Le Nôtre. Le Blond seems the more probable author. James does not appear

[1] See Appendix II.

to have known anything about its authorship,
for the original was published anonymously in
1709 ; but he inclined to think that it was written
by an architect. The translation was published
by subscription of the principal nobility and
gentry of the time. It is illustrated with
excellent engravings of the various parts of the
formal garden, and contains by far the most
valuable account ever published of the system
of garden design as practised by the school of
Le Nôtre. That system was now so completely
matured that it was capable of being reduced
to rules of practice, with the necessary consequence that its break-up was imminent. In
1718 appeared *Ichnographia Rustica, or the
Nobleman's, Gentleman's, and Gardener's Recreations*, by Stephen Switzer, gardener. The
writer of this book evidently supposed that he
was developing the traditions of formal gardening ; but he had, in fact, lost touch of its
essential principle—the principle that the garden
within its enclosure is one thing, and the
landscape outside it another, and that no
attempt should be made to confuse the two.
He devised a system of what he called "rural
and extensive gardening," by which a garden
of 20 acres should look to be 200 or 300.
Walls and fences were to be removed, and
woods and even cornfields made to appear
part of the garden scheme. He urged that
"those large sums of money that have been

buried within the narrow limits of a high wall
upon the trifling and diminutive beauties of
greens and flowers (should be) lightly spread
over great and extensive parks and forests."
The designs which he furnishes are very intricate and tedious. He points out that his
system "cashiers those interlacings of boxwork
and such-like trifling ornaments" (and apparently flowers as well), and there is some ugly
cant about "natural and polite gardening,"
which is ominous of what was to follow.
Indeed, the change was now fairly on the
way. Bridgeman, another well-known gardener
of the time who succeeded Wise as gardener to
George I., abandoned "verdant sculpture," as
Horace Walpole calls it, though he still
trimmed his hedgerows. The abuse and per-
version of the good old custom of pleaching
was a sign of decay. Garden design had reached
the full development of which it was capable
by the end of the seventeenth century ; it was
growing stereotyped ; it became familiar, though
incomprehensible, to the man of letters and the
amateur, and the latter at once set to work to
pull it to pieces.

It now became the fashion to rave about
nature, and to condemn the straightforward
work of the formal school as so much brutal
sacrilege. Pope and Addison led the way, with
about as much love of nature as the elegant
Abbé Delille some three generations later.

Addison began the attack in *The Spectator*,[1] with the following extraordinary argument : — We may assume, he says, that works of nature rise in value according to the degree of their resemblance to works of art. Therefore works of art rise in value according to the degree of their resemblance to nature. Gardens are works of art. Therefore they rise in value according to the degree of their resemblance to nature. Therefore in laying out a garden we are to copy nature as much as possible. This is a concise statement of the whole fallacy of the landscape gardener. In this curious argument the first half of the major premiss begs the question ; we do not value nature by the standard of art ; but even if this was true, the deduction from it of the second proposition is an inference from what is true under conditions to what is true absolutely, and the entire argument based on this amounts to a fallacy of the ambiguous middle, for the term " work of art " is used here both for " works of art " in the ordinary sense and for work which is mechanical, that is made by man as distinct from nature. Pope, the most artificial of writers, followed suit in *The Guardian*[2] with a witty catalogue of objects cut in yew-trees, supposed to be for sale, which included " a St. George in box, his arm scarce long enough, but will be in a condition to stab

[1] *The Spectator*, No. 414, 25th June, 1712.
[2] *The Guardian*, No. 173, 1712.

the Dragon by next April," and "a quickset
hog shot up into a porcupine through being
forgot a week in rainy weather." This was
an excellent sarcasm on an admitted extravagance, and the formal school had undoubtedly
run riot with their pleaching and statuary ; but
this was not so much due to the system as to
the fact that garden design had slipped out of
the hands of cultivated designers and been
monopolised by the nursery gardener. The
latter, as Addison pointed out, would naturally
destroy an old orchard, or anything else, however beautiful, in order to reduce his stock of
evergreens and plants. The "natural" manner
of gardening now became the rage. Pope
turned his 5 acres at Twickenham into a
compendium of nature, and was considered to
have shown admirable taste by condensing
samples of every kind of scenery into a suburban
villa garden. Even the architects were not
true to their colours. Batty Langley published
a sumptuous book on *The New Principles of
Gardening*, the value of which consists chiefly
in its paper and binding ; but Kent, who really
was an architect of ability, was the great rene-
gade. It seems almost inconceivable that a man
such as Kent, who could design fine and severe
architecture, should have lent himself so abjectly
to the fancies of the fashionable amateur. No
doubt he had to make his living, and the fashion
was too strong for him. Kent was something

of a painter as well as an architect, and he set to
work with both hands, as it were, on garden
design ; for while with his T-square and com-
passes he would design indifferently Grecian
temples, Anglo-Saxon ruins, or Gothic churches
for the grounds, he proceeded to form landscape
compositions on the most heroic scale that surely
has ever entered the head of any painter, for the
solid earth was to be his canvas, and the trees
water and rocks his paints. With these materials he endeavoured to the best of his ability to
reproduce the landscapes of Claude and Poussin ;
but he signally failed of his purpose, for instead
of the classical breadth and repose of those great
masters, the whole result was fussiness. According to Sir William Chambers, " Our virtuosi
have scarcely left an acre of shade, or three trees
growing in a line, from the Land's End to the
Tweed." Chambers himself published his *Dis-
sertation on Oriental Gardens* in 1773. This
led, however, to little result beyond the use of
light trellis work for verandahs and the backs
of garden seats. This is how Walpole, most
elegant of gushers, describes Kent's work :
" Selecting favourite objects, and veiling de-
formities by screens of plantations, he realised
the composition of the greatest masters in painting. The living landscape was chastened and
polished, not transformed." The chastening of
nature was rather severe, for we find that it consisted in wholesale destruction of trees, alteration

of ground, building up of rocks, and, for a
crowning effort of genius, in planting dead trees
" to heighten the allusion to natural woods."
He might as well have nailed stuffed nightingales
to the boughs.   As Scott said of him : " His
style is not simplicity, but affectation labouring
to seem simple."   Kent's great work in gardens
was Stowe in Buckinghamshire.   These gardens
were begun by Bridgeman with some approach
to style, but Kent obliterated every trace of it.
He so contrived his views and prospects that
at every turn appeared a fresh *tour de force*.
After inspecting the Hermitage, the Temple
of Venus, the Egyptian Pyramid, and St.
Augustine's Cave, built of roots and moss,
and adorned with indecent inscriptions, the
amazed spectator would proceed to the Saxon
Temple, the Temple of Bacchus, Dido's Cave,
the Witch House, the Temple of Ancient and
Modern Virtue, the Grecian Temple, the Gothic
Temple, and the Palladian Bridge, not to
mention many other monuments of minor
interest, while at every point inscriptions were
at hand to tell you what to admire and to
supply the appropriate sentiments.   Shenstone,
at Leasowes, was even more solicitous for his
visitors, for in places of more than ordinary
interest on his farm he would put a Gothic seat
" still more particularly characterised by an inscription in obsolete language and the black
letter."   This was the practical result of the

process described by Walpole in a sentence, which is probably his masterpiece in claptrap : " Kent leapt the fence and saw that all nature was a garden."

Kent was followed by " Capability " Brown, who began as a kitchen gardener, but took the judicious line that knowledge hampered originality. He accordingly dispensed with any training in design, and rapidly rose to eminence. Brown's notion of a landscape consisted of a park encircled by a belt of trees, a piece of ornamental water, and a clump—the latter indispensable ; and on these lines he proceeded to cut down avenues and embellish nature with the utmost aplomb. He died in 1783, and was succeeded by Humphrey Repton and other professors of landscape gardening, who between them irrevocably destroyed some of the finest gardens in England. Two instances will show the taste of these men. One of them advised, as an improvement to Powis Castle, that a precipitous rock in front of the Castle with a stone balustraded terrace and stairs should be blown up, in order to make a uniform grassy slope to the Castle ; and in Repton's *Landscape Gardening* appears the following remark : " The motley appearance of red bricks with white stone, by breaking the unity of effect, will often destroy the magnificence of the most splendid compositions," and he accordingly recommends that the bricks should be covered with plaster

and stone colour.   The unutterable dulness of
the English Country House of the early part of
the last century is suggested here in all its weari-
some pedantry.   The effort aimed at seems to
have been a sort of correct respectability of
colour, something which should not violate de-
corum.   The garden front of Hampton Court
is a sufficient answer to such a grotesque assertion.   The principles of landscape gardening,
or rather certain assumptions which do duty for
principles, were first formulated by Thomas
Wheatly, in his *Observations on Modern Gardening*, published in 1776, which became the standard
book on the *Jardin Anglais*, and has, so far as
any theory is concerned, remained so ever since.
Wheatly further signalised himself by completely
destroying the remains of the formal gardens at
Nonsuch in 1786.   Horace Walpole published
an *Essay on Modern Gardening* in 1785, in
which he repeated what other writers had said
on the subject.   This was at once translated
and had a great circulation on the continent.[1]
The *Jardin à l' Anglaise* became the rage ; many
beautiful old gardens were destroyed in France

---

[1] The *Jardin à l'Anglaise* was purely and simply what is now known
as landscape gardening—a term which betrays its origin in the latter
part of the eighteenth century.   Certain writers have spoken of the
landscape garden as " The English Garden," but in point of fact till the
middle of the eighteenth century a view of garden design precisely
opposed to this prevailed in England as well as in other civilised countries
of Europe.   So far, therefore, as history goes, the older, that is the formal
garden, has the real claim to be called the English garden.   Curiously
enough, Taine (*Voyage en Italie*), in a sketch of the Villa Albani, con-
fuses the *Jardin Anglais* with the older garden.

and elsewhere, and Scotch and English gardeners were in demand all over Europe to renovate gardens in the English manner. It is not an exhilarating thought that in the one instance in which English taste in a matter of design has taken hold on the Continent, it has done so with such disastrous results.

It is not to be supposed, however, that this new view of gardening took immediate and complete possession of England. Fashions travelled slowly in the eighteenth century, and many a formal garden in provincial towns and country places was laid out in the older style as late as the beginning of the nineteenth century. The terrace and great staircase of Prior Park, near Bath, designed by Wood, the architect, is one of the finest examples still in existence in England of garden architecture ; and the terrace at Brympton, in Somersetshire, is said to have been constructed in the early part of last century. Moreover, men of real cultivation began to resent the destruction of places which for them, at least, were instinct with scholarly associations, and the cant and fallacies of the landscapist were too transparent to pass unchallenged. Sir Uvedale Price, a man of independent views and considerable intelligence, was perhaps the first to see the error of his ways. In his essay on *The Decorations near the House*, he tells of an old garden of his own, in two divisions, all walled in, with terraces and summer-house and rich wrought-iron gates. This garden he destroyed, with no pleasure to himself, as he confesses, and with no motive except that of being in the fashion. He says that he succeeded at much expense in making his grounds like anybody else's and like the fields outside, but lost for ever the seclusion, the charm, the distinction of his old-fashioned garden. Price advocated a threefold division — the garden immediately round the house was to be formal, the garden beyond to be in the landscape style, and the park to be left to itself. His idea was that the transition should be gradual, and this idea was worked upon by Sir Charles Barry in laying out the gardens of Trentham Hall and other places. This, however, seems to me to show a misapprehension of the intention of the formal garden as a matter of design. Instead of the transition being gradual, there should be no question where the garden ends. As Price himself pointed out, half the charm of the older garden was its contrast with the surrounding scenery, the clean line of demarcation given by a good brick wall, or at least an iron railing on a low brick plinth, with the background of the trees beyond. As for the vaunted ha-ha, it is little better than a silly practical joke, and in point of fact was not invented by Kent at all, but was known to the French designers of the seventeenth century, for the ha-ha is named and described as a common feature in gardens in

The Theory and Practice of Gardening, 1712. The last word of protest was written by Sir Walter Scott. In 1827 he wrote a paper on " Gardens " for *The Quarterly*, which appeared in 1828 as a review of Sir Henry Stewart's *Planter's Guide*. In this he pointed out the irreparable folly of destroying these formal gardens, and the fallacy of claiming for landscape gardening that it was loyal to nature ; or that Milton, who of all men loved the formal garden, was in any sense identified with the introduction of landscape gardening. The paper contains a charming description of the garden of Barncluith, in Lanarkshire, an old garden of the eighteenth century laid out by one of the Millars, "full of long straight walks, betwixt hedges of yew and hornbeam, which rose tall and close on every side." Scott also describes an old garden at Kelso which he first saw in 1783. In his journal for 29th August 1827 he notes that "the yew hedges, labyrinths, wildernesses . . . are all obliterated, and the place is as common and vulgar as may be. In 1829 Felton published his *Gleanings on Gardens*. Since that date the question of garden design seems to have lost interest for the public. An article appeared in *The Quarterly* in 1842 on London's *Encyclopædia*, and a paper in *The Carthusian* for 1845. The writer of the latter essay supported the old formal garden with a wealth of scholarly allusion, and the same ground was taken up by Mrs.

BARNCLUITH · LANARKSHIRE

Fig. 17.

Francis Foster in a charming little book called *The Art of Gardening*, published in 1881, and in the well-known writings of E. V. B. Until quite recently little attention has been paid to the formal garden.[1] The landscape gardener has had it all his own way, so much so that he has ceased to think it necessary to lavish that abuse on the formal school which used to be the regular preface to his dissertations. Some very successful attempts, however, in formal gardens have been made within the last forty years. Arley and Penshurst are well-known instances. The latter was laid out by Lord Delisle, and is perhaps one of the most beautiful gardens in England or anywhere else. Of contemporary designers it would be unbecoming to speak, but the late George Devey and W. Eden-Nesfield ought to be mentioned as architects who made a deliberate and very successful effort to design the house and grounds in relation to each other, and this principle, carrying with it the full appreciation of the formal method of gardening, is now generally accepted by those who consider that architecture is a fine art, and not a mere matter of business or building police.

Looking generally at the history of gardening in England, one cannot but admit that the disappearance of formal gardening and the

---

[1] Since the date when this was written (1892) several writers have dealt with gardens, and a valuable series of illustrations, " Gardens Old and New," has been issued by the proprietors of *Country Life*.

chaos which followed was due to the abuse of the system itself. The note of warning uttered by Rea and Worlidge was not heeded. The designer became so intent on showing his skill in design that he forgot that a garden is a place for real flowers and grass, and not for conventional flowers mapped out on the ground in different coloured sands. Some of the designs for parterres in James's translation are melancholy instances of perverted taste. Formal gardening fell into its dotage, and the vanity of technique overpowered the reserve and sobriety and genuine love of nature which guided the earlier masters, and this was the justification, in fact, of the violent change that occurred in the eighteenth century. But the change was thrust upon us by people who not only had no sympathy with the older system, but by their absence of training were quite unqualified to judge whether that system was good or bad. The consequence was that the good went down with the bad, and the fundamental principle of the relation between the garden and the house was completely lost sight of, though that principle had been accepted as a matter of course throughout all the greatest periods of English art.

GARDEN AND TERRACE: MONTACUTE: SOMERSET:

CHAPTER V

THE COURTS, TERRACES, WALKS

THE advice given by the earlier seventeenth-century writers as to sites does not precisely agree with the instances still in existence. Markham, in his *Country Farm*, advises that the house and garden should be placed on high ground, just under the brow of a hill for preference, with an east aspect, or a south aspect "borrowing somewhat of the east, for the winds blowing from those quarters are drie, more hot than cold, but very wholesome, as

well for the body as for the spirit of man."
Thomas Hill had already made the astounding
statement that the east wind is hotter than the
west, simply transcribing from Latin and Italian
writers.   Both writers advise against placing
the house on low ground, or near moats or
standing water.   Lawson, however, advised
that the orchard should be planted on low
ground by a river, and this was repeatedly done
in the sixteenth and seventeenth centuries.
Great noblemen's houses, such as Wollaton,
Bolsover, and Hardwick, were sometimes built
on the tops of hills, but men of lesser means
seem to have liked the shelter of low-lying
ground, and the custom of placing the house on
the highest and most conspicuous part of the
estate was not fully established till the end of
the eighteenth century.

Markham's arrangement of house and grounds
has been described in the second chapter, and
the general principle of it remained unaltered
till the introduction of landscape gardening.
In front of the house was the fore court, walled
in on every side, with an entrance in the centre,
opposite the door of the house ; on one side
was the base court, or bass court, as it came to
be called, which included all the stables and
farm - buildings ; on the other side were the
pleasure gardens, with a terrace along the side
of the house, as at Montacute, and at the back
of the house the fruit and kitchen gardens.

This arrangement, however, was by no means universal. The fore court and one or more bass courts nearly always existed, but their relative positions were modified to suit the necessities of the site. In old prints and drawings it is not always easy to classify the courts. James, in his *Theory of Gardening*, distinguishes between the fore court, the castle court or house court, and the bass courts, and this is a very convenient classification. The house court is the court immediately in front of the house, surrounded on three sides by the centre block and two wings of the house. The fore court is the court or courts in front of this, giving access from the entrance to the house court. The bass courts are the courts to the right or left of the fore court, or on both sides of it, or even at the back of the house, comprising the stables and inferior buildings. Kip's views show several different arrangements of the courts. The house court was usually paved over its entire surface, or two square grass plots were left with broad flagged paths round the sides and down the middle. This court was raised above the fore court, and separated from it by a balustrade or an iron railing on a dwarf wall, with a flight of steps opposite the central path. Fine instances existed at Badminton and Newnham Paddox, in Warwickshire, and at Bretby, in Derbyshire, now destroyed. Kip's view of the latter shows a wide paved path the full width of

the centre bay of the façade, with grass plots
on either side spaced out with standard-trees
in cases. At Althorp the house court was
separated from the fore court by a moat, with
a bridge opposite the outer entrance to the
fore court. In some instances, and particularly
in the case of houses built after the middle of
the seventeenth century, a terrace running
along the front of the façade took the place of
the house court, as at Chatsworth before it was
altered, Wrest House, in Bedfordshire, Wimple,
in Cambridgeshire, and the house of Sir W.
Blackett at Newcastle (Kip, 54) ; and eventually,
as the quadrangular plan for the house was
abandoned, and the long symmetrical façade
superseded the H or half ⊓ plan, the house
court slipped out of use, and the fore court was
brought up immediately in front of the entrance
door of the house, as in old Burlington House
(Kip, 29). Few instances remain of the house
court proper, owing to the inconvenience of
having to walk a considerable distance from the
carriage to the front door ; but examples of
what are practically house courts still exist in
old almshouses, as, for instance, in the almshouse
at Etwall, in Derbyshire.

The fore court lasted well into the eighteenth
century. The simplest form of a fore court is
a square walled-in enclosure in front of the
entrance door, with a gateway in the centre of
the wall to the road, and either buildings or

plain walls on either side. There were usually
pavilions of more or less importance in the
angles next the road. There is a comparatively
perfect instance of a simple fore court at Wootton
Lodge, in Staffordshire. The carriage-road
sweeps round a circular grass plot up to a grand
flight of twenty-five steps to the entrance door.
This arrangement of a plain circular or oval plot
of grass in the centre of the court, with a fountain or statue in the middle, was very generally
used in the seventeenth century ; but Switzer,
writing in 1718, says that the custom was being
abandoned, because it diminished the space available for coaches, and the courts were more often
paved with different coloured stones laid
chequerwise, or in circular or star-shaped
designs. In the smaller houses the fore court
was simply a square enclosure, with a paved path
from the gate to the front door. There is an
excellent instance in existence at Eyam Hall, in
Derbyshire. On the left is the road to the
offices, on the right the gardens. A small
terrace with a low wall raised eight steps above
the fore court runs in front of the house out to
a door in the right-hand wall, by which access
is given to the garden down a flight of five
semicircular steps. A good view of a small
fore court is given in Kennett's *Parochial
Antiquities* (1695) view of Saresden Hall, since
destroyed. The fore courts of these smaller
houses are not always easy to discover. As a

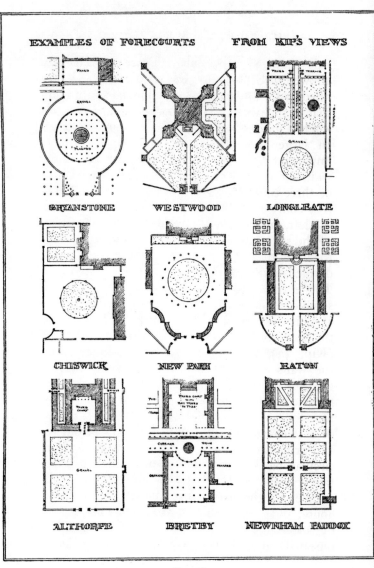

EXAMPLES OF FORECOURTS — FROM KIP'S VIEWS

BRYANSTONE — WESTWOOD — LONGLEATE

CHISWICK — NEW PARK — EATON

ALTHORPE — BRETBY — NEWNHAM PADDOX

Fig. 18.

rule they only exist where the house has been allowed to decay, and the court is so abundantly filled with apple-trees and gooseberry bushes, that it appears as nothing more than an ordinary kitchen garden in front of a tumbledown house. In larger houses the fore court was a very important feature. It extended at least the full width of the façade, but sometimes it was twice or three times that length. There was a grand fore court at Althorp, flanked by the stables on the left, and the gardens on the right ; the whole of the space in front of the house was gravelled ; to the right and left of this were two grass plots divided and surrounded by broad gravel paths. The entrance was usually in the centre, but in some cases, as in the Earl of Burlington's house at Chiswick (Kip, 30), the entrance was placed to one corner. At New Park, in Surrey (Kip, 33), the entrance was in the centre, but the walls on either side, instead of continuing the line of the gates, formed the side walls by reversed curves. At Bretby, in Derbyshire, the fore court was oblong, running the whole length of base court, house, and garden, with iron gates and grilles at each end, and a fountain in a semi-circular bay opposite the centre of the house ; a raised walk with a row of polled trees ran parallel to the fore court on the side to the house, and was separated from the house court by an iron grille. The fore court was often repeated, so that there were two or three fore

Fig. 19.—Saresden, from Kennett.

courts ; at Newnham Paddox there were three
such courts with gateways leading from one to
the other.   At Orchard Portman there was an
outer fore court separated from the inner fore
court by a wall and two-storey gatehouse.
Kip's view of the old gardens at Longleat
shows a very remarkable fore court.   The outer
court was only separated from the park by a
fence, with a wrought-iron gateway leading to
the fore court proper.   A broad flagged causeway
led from the gates to the front door, with flights
of fifteen steps leading to a lower terrace on
either side in front of the house.   The sides of
this causeway were formed apparently with grass
slopes ; on either side of it were grass lawns at a
lower level than the terrace, with circular basins
and fountains in the centre.   The effect of such
an arrangement must have been quite magnificent.   The whole of it was swept away by
Capability Brown ; and the utter insignificance of
the present approach shows the full capacity for
mischief of the landscape system.   At old Eaton
Hall the outer court was formed by a semicircular wall, extending beyond the full width
of the inner fore court sufficiently far to admit
of gateways into the base courts on either side
of the inner fore court.   This is a simple and
masterly plan.   The fore court at Westwood, in
Worcestershire, was laid out lozenge-wise, with
a gatehouse in the centre and three-storey
pavilions at the two angles.   These instances

are enough to show that the fore court was not tied down to one uniform plan, but might be varied indefinitely to meet the conditions of the house and grounds. The house court was abandoned for the practical reason that it prevented a carriage drawing up at the front door ; but no such objection holds against the fore court. It gives privacy to the house, and when properly planned, provides a convenient means of grouping the stables and outbuildings with the main block of the house. Existing instances show that there is no reason why it should not be applied to small country houses as well as to big ones. Nothing can be meaner than the carriage-drive and rhododendron bed which usually form a miserable apology for a fore court proper. The advantages of a fore court where the ground is shut in by a road in front and buildings at the sides are obvious.

The terrace is admitted, even by the landscapist, to be desirable near the house. In the first place, it presents to the eye a solid foundation for the house to start from, and gives the house itself greater importance by raising it above the level of the adjacent grounds, and again it is healthier. There is something uncomfortable in the idea of a house placed flat on the ground or down in a hole. It need not necessarily be damp, but one always imagines that it will, and that the timber will decay, and the plaster moulder, and rats run over the floor ;

but when the house starts from a terrace it at
least looks dry, and the terrace enables you to
see the garden. The French author of *The
Theory of Gardening* lays it down that there
should always be a descent from the building to
the garden of three steps at least. The main
terrace was always placed to overlook the principal garden. This might be either to the back
of the house or to the left or right of it, according to circumstance. It has been given as a rule
for the width of such a terrace that it should
be equal to the height of the house from the
ground line to the eaves. This rule is so far
good that it is likely to prevent those *petites
manières mesquines*, against which the French
author warned designers, but it is not borne out
by existing instances. The great terrace at
Montacute, which overlooks the west garden,
is about 45 feet wide, which is much less than
the height of the building. On the other hand,
the north terrace at Versailles measures about
120 feet wide by 820 long; the terrace at
Bolsover, in Derbyshire, about 300 feet long
by 50 feet wide. The proportions of a terrace
depend not only on the height of the building,
but on the length of the terrace itself. In
Marshal Tallard's garden the house terrace
was 60 feet long by 14 wide. Switzer says the
house terrace can hardly be too wide, and that,
as a rule, in England they were much too
narrow. He gives a plan of a terrace 100 feet

wide, but as it was to be divided into ten strips
of grass, gravel, and paving, it can hardly be
considered a terrace so much as a terrace garden.
For the side terrace, he says, the width should
not be less than 20 feet or more than 40.   In
The Theory of Gardening, a terrace, shown on
the third plate, scales 40 feet wide to 190 feet
long, which is not a very happy proportion.
It is impossible to lay down any definite rule
for the proportions of a terrace, but, generally
speaking, the tendency is to make them too
narrow.   Another important consideration is
the height of the terrace above the garden.
On sloping ground this will probably determine
itself ; but where the terrace is almost entirely
artificial, it is not much use making the level of
the terrace less than 2 to 3 feet above the
garden, and, for effect, the higher the better,
within certain limits.   Where, however, the fall
of the ground is very sudden, it is best to make
the terrace in two levels—that is, an upper and
a lower terrace, communicating by flights of
stairs.   At Kingston House, Bradford-on-
Avon, the difficulty is got over in a very skilful
way.   The house is raised 12.0 above the
lower garden ; in front of the house is a terrace
24 feet wide, with a flight of fourteen steps in
the centre, descending to a grass platform with
mitred slopes.   The path runs to right and left,
and descends to the lower garden by flights of
seven steps ; off this path, on either side of the

A TERRACED GARDEN : KINGSTON HOUSE : BRADFORD-ON-AVON

Fig. 20.

terrace walls, two steps ascend to grass terraces,
27 feet wide and 52 paces and 29 paces long
respectively, which run under the walls of the
upper gardens to right and left of the house.
The terrace should be made with a slight fall
away from the house of about $1\frac{1}{4}$ inches in 10
feet.

The side of the terrace to the garden may
be formed either with brickwork or masonry,
or with a grass slope. Details of the first
will be given under the head of Garden Architecture. Where a grass slope is used, the
point to aim at is to keep the verge of the
terrace well defined, and to ensure this the
slope of the bank should form an unmistak-
able angle with the ground both at its top
and its base. A gradually curved slope is
useless ; it defeats the whole purpose of the
terrace by merging it into the garden, and
where the landscape gardener uses a slope he
makes it much too flat. Switzer gave $2\frac{1}{2}$ horizontal to 1 perpendicular for the slope, on the
ground that anything steeper than this cannot
be mowed or rolled. This is a useful proportion, and admits of a staircase at the same angle
as the slope of the bank, with steps of 6 inches
rise and 15 inches tread ; flights of steps at a
steeper angle than this are unsatisfactory out of
doors, except under special conditions. The
proportion generally used by the French
gardeners of the seventeenth century was $\frac{2}{3}$ to

1 [1]—that is, $\frac{2}{3}$ of the height for the horizontal length of the slope ; but it was also made on the diagonal of the square, and in some cases at an angle still more obtuse, in order to prevent the moisture running off too quickly, and save the grass along the top from withering in summer. As a matter of fact, these slopes are too steep to be practicable in England— the grass will not grow satisfactorily except on a rather flat slope, and if it does it is a difficult matter to keep it trim. Moreover, when it comes to the steps all sorts of difficulties arise in the attempt to reconcile the angle of the steps with the angle of the bank. If the terrace involves much made ground along the outer edge, care must be taken to build up the earth, to prevent its slipping down. *The Theory of Gardening* advises the following practice :— " After having laid the earth 1 foot high, beginning at bottom, you must spread upon it a bed of Fascines, or Hurdles (made of willow), 6 foot wide, in rows one against another, and dispose them so that the great ends or roots may lie next the face of the slope, and come within a foot of the surface ; then lay another bed of earth upon this, and continue the same to the top. Over this wattled work you lay the turf, after covering it with a little earth." A method of strengthening banks somewhat similar

---

[1] *The Theory and Practice of Gardening.*

to this is recommended by William Lawson. The terrace next the house was either gravelled or paved. A splendid instance of a paved terrace, the full width of the garden, existed at Longleat, and several others are shown in Kip.

Besides the terrace next the house, a terrace was often formed parallel to it at the opposite

FIG. 21.—Hales Place.[1]

end of the garden. In the earlier gardens of the seventeenth century this was almost invariably done. In the gardens described and figured by Markham and Lawson, the " mount," or raised walk at the end of the garden, with garden-houses at either end, was an indispensable feature. There is a good example of this in

[1] Hales Place, or Place House, Tenterden, was a seat of the Hales family. It is now a farm-house, and is usually called Place House.

ruins, dating from the middle of the sixteenth
century, at Place House, near Tenterden, in
Kent. The garden, which is all walled in,
measures 47 paces wide by 92 long. It is
now a grass field. At the end of the garden
opposite to the house is a raised walk with
brick retaining wall on the garden side, and
a wall 8.0 high on the outer side of the walk.
The walk is 16 feet wide, 5.0 high above
the garden level, and 41 paces long. It is
reached by a flight of nine steps in the centre
from the garden. At each end of the walk
are octagonal garden-houses in two storeys,
the ground floor entered from the garden. On
six sides of the houses there are two light
windows with four-centred heads. The ground
floor is paved with bricks ; the first floor has a
wood floor, and the walls are plastered. All
the details are in brick, with mouldings worked
in plaster to look like stone, and evidently date
from before the middle of the sixteenth century.
At Brickwall, in Sussex, there is a grass walk 9
feet wide and about 130 feet long, with seats at
either end, which separates the garden from the
park ; this is raised six steps above the garden.
At Rycott, in Oxfordshire, there existed a magnificent raised walk along the top of a one-storey
building, surmounted by a balustrade. This
was reached by double flights of steps from the
garden, with an elaborate pavilion raised on the
terrace opposite the steps. Every vestige of

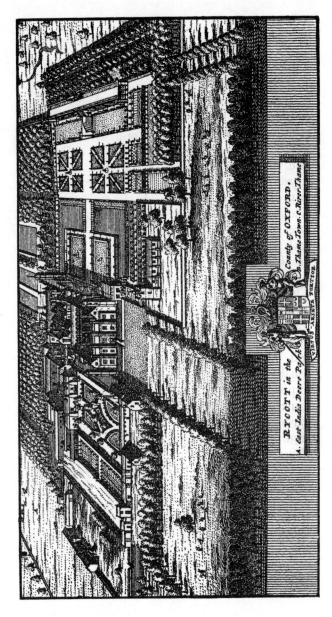

RYCOTT in the County of OXFORD.
A. East India Deere Park. B. Thame Town. C. River Tham.

Fig. 22.

this garden has disappeared but one old cedar. The terrace was frequently continued round the two remaining sides of the garden, so that a commanding view of the garden is got from every side, as at Montacute.   In this garden the terrace next the house has a wall on the garden side.   The other three terraces are formed with a grass slope to the gardens and flights of steps in the centre of every side.   At Brickwall there is a rather unusual variation.   There is no terrace in front of the house, but a paved brick path with flights of six steps at either end communicates with a raised walk 8.9 wide, which runs round the other three sides of the garden. The garden itself is raised three steps above the level of the path in front of the house.   Raised walks, as described above, are shown in Logan's views of Corpus Christi, Cambridge, and Balliol and Oriel at Oxford.   Bowling-greens were usually surrounded by raised terraces, and in important gardens terraces or causeways were sometimes laid out across the middle of the garden to enable the parterres to be properly seen.   There is a good instance of this in the Privy Garden at Hampton Court, also at Packwood, and at Ven House in Somerset.   Switzer says these terraces should be raised between 2.6 and 3.6 above the garden.   The terrace at Risley, in Derbyshire, is at some distance from the house, and runs along one side of the garden and beyond it.   The terrace is separated from

THE TERRACE: RUSLEY FALL: DERBYSHIRE

Fig. 23.

the garden by a long narrow piece of water, which was probably dug out to form the terrace. The terrace rises some 9 feet above this water, with a retaining wall of masonry and a heavy stone balustrade above it. It is reached from the garden by a flight of seven steps rising over the bridge, with a rather elaborate stone gateway. The terrace is 289 paces long, and is in two levels. That next the balustrade is 14 feet wide and gravelled. Above this is a grass walk, 25 feet wide, with box-hedges, and a ha-ha on the side to the park. Part of the balustrade has been removed, and now encloses the playground of the Grammar School.

The terraces hitherto described are such as might be made in ground with a slight fall. Hanging gardens are a form of terrace, but it is best to distinguish the two. The terrace is specifically a walk raised above the adjacent ground, with a certain proportion between the length and width, whereas a hanging garden is in the nature of a raised platform, which may be as broad as it is long, or any other width and any height.[1] These hanging gardens were going out of fashion in Worlidge's time, probably because of their great expense in making ; but in certain cases they were rendered necessary by the ground. Camden says of Holdenby House,

---

[1] The distinction can be well seen at Penshurst, where, in front of the house, there is a broad platform of turf raised above the garden level, and the terrace proper runs down one side of the garden.

built for Hatton in 1583 : " Above all is especially to be noted with what industry and toyle of
man the garden hath been raised, levelled, and
formed out of a most craggye and unprofitable
piece of ground, now framed a most pleasant,
sweete, and princely place." The gardens of
Haddon Hall are well known. They are laid out
in four main levels ; at the top is a raised walk
70 paces long by 15 wide, planted with a double
row of lime-trees. About 10 feet below this is
the yew-tree terrace, divided into three plots,
about 15 yards square, surrounded by stone
curbs, with yew-trees in each angle. These
were once clipped, but are now grown into
great trees overshadowing the entire terrace.
Dorothy Vernon's stairs descend on to this
yew-tree terrace. A flight of twenty-six steps
led from this terrace to a lower garden about
40 yards square, divided into two grass plots.
A walk from this garden skirted round two
sides of a second garden laid out in three
levels, and reached the postern door in the outer
garden-wall by seventy-one steps laid out in
seven consecutive flights. The original gardens
at Chatsworth were laid out as a succession of
terrace gardens, but the greater part of this
was destroyed by Paxton. " Queen Mary's
Bower," at Chatsworth, is a curious instance of
what must be called a hanging garden ; it is a
square enclosure on a raised platform, with
retaining walls and open parapet surrounded by

a moat. This was probably a garden of herbs.
Kip's view of New Park, in Surrey, shows a
large garden, cut out in the side of a hill, with
a high double embankment above it, and an
embankment in three levels below. The house
stood at the bottom of the hill. This is an
exceedingly foolish arrangement. The garden
would be invisible from the house except to a
person standing on the top of the chimney. If
you must have hanging gardens, it is better, as
Worlidge pointed out, to have them below the
house than above it, and not to put the terraces
too close together—that is to say, to keep the
level pieces (what the French used to call the
Plein pied) as wide as possible, otherwise you
are in a constant state of going up and down
stairs. There are good examples of combined
terrace and bank work at Clevedon Court in
Somerset, and in the garden of St. Catherine's
Court, Bath. In *The Theory of Gardening* a third
method of dealing with sloping ground is given.
This dispensed with terraces and left the ground
on a slope, but provided at intervals elaborate
landing-places, called generally " amphitheatres "
with " easy ascents and flights of steps for com-
munication, with front paces, counter-terraces,
volutes, rolls, banks, and slopes of grass, placed
and disposed with symmetry," and further
adorned with figures and fountains. This was
considered in France the most magnificent way
of dealing with a slope, but it was seldom

adopted in England. Such a treatment would
be exceedingly costly to carry out and maintain,
in decent order.

The dislike of regular design entertained by
the landscape gardener is shown most conspicu-
ously in his treatment of paths. He lays them
about at random, and keeps them so narrow that
they look like threads, and there is barely room
to walk abreast, and he makes a particular point
of planting trees and bushes in the way, to give
him an opportunity of winding his path, and
then taking credit to himself for subordinating
his paths to " nature." The width and proportion of paths and their relation to the amount
of turf on either side is a point of the greatest
importance in garden design. In the seventeenth
century it was taken for granted that all paths
should be straight. Lawson says "One principall
end of orchards is recreation by walks, and
universallie walks are straight," and the main
walks of the garden were always wide enough
at the least for two or three people to walk
abreast. Markham gives 14 feet as a minimum
width for main paths. He advises that the
alleys be made in three divisions—a broad walk
in the middle, 7 or 8 feet wide at the least,
covered with sand or small gravel, or even fine
coal-dust, and on either side a width of grass
of the same width as the centre alley. Thus,
the sandy walk being 7 feet wide, the entire
alley, including the grass on either side, will be

21 feet across.   Markham notices that the
French paved or tiled their centre paths, but
he preferred our gravel.   The centre path is
to be slightly raised in the centre to throw off
wet.   A useful caution is given by Meager
(1670) that the fall to either side from the
centre should be so slight as to be hardly dis-
cernible, for "a great fall is unhandsome, and
uneasie for such as wear high-heeled shoes."
Markham gives as practical reasons for his
triple walk—(1) That the contrast of colours, of
the green of the grass and the yellow of the
sand, is delightful to the eye, for "beauty is
nothing but an excellent mixture or consent of
colours, as in the composition of a delicate
woman, the grace of her cheeke is the mixture
of red and white, the wonder of her eye, blacke
and white, and the beauty of her hand blew and
white"; (2) if your walks are all grass, you
trample down part by treading on it, and make
it shabby and ill-favoured; (3) that after dew
and rain you cannot walk on it at all.   Another
form of triple walk is given by Worlidge, who
classifies walks under three heads.   (1) The
best, he says, are made with stone "about the
breadth of 5 foot in the midst of a gravel walk
of about 5 or 6 feet gravel on each side the
stone, or of grasse, which you please."   (2)
Gravel walks.   These are good to be laid out
under fruit walls, because they reflect the sun
better than grass, and should be made in the

following manner :—Remove all the surface
earth and all roots from the subsoil for a depth
of 8 or 9 inches. Fill in with coarse unscreened
gravel (or broken bricks) for 5 or 6 inches,
level and well ram it, and lay over the surface a
final coat of fine gravel 2 or 3 inches thick.
If moss appears, you are to rake up the top
coat and roll it again. To prevent the earth
at the sides from mixing with the gravel and
causing weeds and moss, the sides should be
supported with two or three courses of brickwork, or bricks set on end, edge to edge,
the top of the bricks to be about an inch
below the surface. To prevent the gravel
disintegrating in frost, a coating of sea-shells
or brick refuse broken up fine is useful. On
either side of the gravel walk verges of turf
should be formed for use in hot weather ; the
grass may be separated from the gravel by stone
edging rising 3 or 4 inches above the surface
of the path.[1] Switzer gives a rule for the
section of the path. It should be 1 inch rise
to 5 feet in width ; thus if a path is 20 feet
wide, it ought to be 4 inches higher in the
middle than at the sides. (3) Green walks,
made either by laying turf or by "raking them
fine and sowing them with hay-dust or seed,
which may be had at the bottom of a hay-mow."

[1] In the quadrangle of New College, Oxford, the oval of turf is
raised some 3 to 4 inches above the gravel ; a small stone curb rises
2 inches or so above the gravel, and the edge of the turf is flush with its
face. By this means a perfectly true edge is kept.

They should be very slightly rounded at the
top, and have a water table on either side 2
to 3 inches deep.   The flower garden described
by Worlidge practically consisted of three such
paths as the last, with flower-beds between.   It
was to be oblong in shape, forming the centre
third of a square, of which the other two-thirds
were occupied by the kitchen gardens and
orchard.   The flower garden was to consist of
a broad gravel walk, with borders of flowers,
with green walks beyond these borders, and
borders of perennials planted between the green
walks and the palisades.

London and Wise, in *The Retired Gard'ner*,
say that in a garden of 4 acres the main path
parallel to the house should be at least 20
feet wide, the path down the centre and the
walks at the sides and ends 15 feet, and intermediate paths 12 feet wide ; all alleys should
have a border of grass or flowers 3 feet wide
on either side, and they add, in a note, " We
generally make our alleys 2 foot broad for
passing, 5 foot for wheeling, and 7 foot for two
persons to walk abreast in."   " Walks " are
dealt with in some detail in *The Theory of
Gardening*.   The author distinguishes between
" single walks," with a single row of trees or
a palisade on either side, and " double walks,"
which consisted of a broad walk in the middle,
with smaller walks at the sides.   The side
walks were separated from the centre walks by

a line of single trees, and from the grounds by
a palisade breast high. These side walks were
called counter walks. They were usually made
half the width of the centre walk. For instance,
if the entire walk was 48 feet wide, the centre
walk would be 24 feet wide, the side walks 12
feet each ; but the counter walks should never
be less than 6 feet wide at the least. " The
best way to gravel walks," he continues, " is to
make a bed of mason's rubble or stone dust,
lay at the bottom 7 or 8 inches thickness of
the coarser stone or gallets, and upon that about
2 inches thickness of the finest dust that has
been run through a sieve. Let this be beaten
three several times with the Beater, after having
been well watered each time, and then spread
the gravel upon it, which also should be well
beaten. When you lay a bed of saltpetre over
this mason's dust, as is done in making a mall
or Base to bowl on, it should be beat eight or
nine times." Coarse gravel or pebbles may be
used instead of mason's dust. He admits that
this way of gravelling is " very chargeable," and
that in ordinary cases 2 inches of gravel well
beaten and rolled may do. " Draining wells
should be made at convenient distances of flint
and dug stones." Another method is to make
a deep V groove under the length of the path,
and fill up with boulders and smaller stones to
form a continuous drain. As to the dimensions
of great walks, the French author gives a width

of from 30 to 36 feet for a walk 600 feet long,
42 to 48 for 1200 feet, 54 to 60 for 1800
feet, and so on.   The Broad Walk at Hampton
Court, as laid out by Wise in 1699, was 2264
feet long by 39 feet wide.

Fig. 24.—From *The Gardener's Labyrinth*.

Besides the main walks of the garden there
are the small paths between beds and parterres.
In *The Gardener's Labyrinth* 3 or 4 feet is
given as the width for such an alley covered
with sand, and 1 foot as the width for the
cross path between the beds.   One foot to 1

foot 6 inches continued to be a common width
for the paths inside parterres down to the end
of the eighteenth century. At Bellair, in King's
County, Ireland, there is a parterre of clipped
box along the upper side of the kitchen garden
in which the width is 16 inches. This was laid
out in 1790. Rea gives a few particulars of the
alleys to the fret of his flower garden. These were
to be 2 feet 6 inches between the fret, gravelled
and rolled and separated from the beds by a
rail 5 inches by $1\frac{1}{4}$ thick, carefully gauged and
levelled and painted white, kept in position by
stout wooden pins about 18 inches long, nailed
to the rail and driven into the ground. The
rail was to be 4 inches above the surface of the
path and the grass 1 inch. This rule for the
height of the grass above the path is still given
by landscape gardeners. The small alleys
running in and out of the different parts of the
fret communicated with a broad path 17 feet 6
inches wide, running round the four sides of the
entire fret. Instead of the plank, Rea says box-
edging will do for a border to beds and grass,
but all the borders to the walks should be set
with these planks.

A charming walk is described by Lawson in
dealing with the fences of his orchard. The
best fence, he says, is a hedge with a mount or
double ditch ; the ditches are to be 2 yards wide
and 4 feet deep. Between them is to be formed
a walk 6 feet wide, raised some 5 or 6 feet

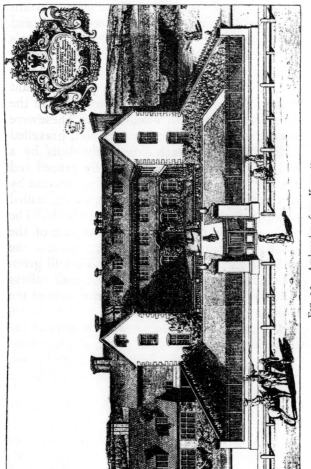

FIG. 25.—Ambrosden, from Kennett.

above the level of the orchard or garden. The
outer bank of this walk is to be planted with
thorn, the inner with cherry, plum, damson,
bullas, or filbert, and the trees to be trimmed
to any form you fancy. At each corner of the
walk and in the middle of each side "a mound
would be raysed, whereabout the woode might
claspe, powdered with woodebinde." There is
an orchard at the Lordship House, Hadham,
in Hertfordshire, which closely follows this idea,
and was probably laid out early in the seventeenth
century. The orchard, which is rectangular, is
surrounded by a moat (now dry), and beyond
this, on either side, are raised grass walks
with old yew hedges. The effect is extremely
good. Switzer mentions a terrace walk at the
end of a garden 12 to 20 feet wide, 2 to 3 feet
above the garden, with a parapet wall on the
outer side, and a graft or ditch to separate it
from the park 15 feet wide and 5 deep. This
sounds rather bare and uninviting after Lawson's
beautiful idea.

VIEW OF FORECOURT SHEWING ONE OF THE PAVILIONS : MONTACUTE :

CHAPTER VI

KNOTS, PARTERRES, GRASS-WORK, MOUNTS, BOWLING-GREENS, THEATRES

THE ordinary modern flower-bed is ugly in form
and monotonous in colour, and it seems to be
thought necessary to border it with the ugly
lobelia, regardless of the colours of the flower-
bed itself. All the fancy has gone out of it,
and little or no attempt is made to lay out
the beds on any consecutive scheme. Contrast
this with the beds of the old gardens of New
College, now destroyed.[1] In front of the
entrance gateway there was a broad path about
18 feet wide, with cross paths subdividing the
garden into four square plots. On the right-
hand plot as you entered was worked, probably
in rosemary, hyssop, or thyme, the arms of New
College and the motto " manners makyth man "
and the date. In the next plot was a curious
device in flowers. On the left hand was planted
the royal arms and the date 1628 ; and the

---

[1] Logan's *Oxonia Illustrata.*

plot beyond was laid out as an enormous sun-dial, the hours probably shown in box or rosemary on an oval of sand, with an upright dial formed of wood in the centre. Olivier de Serres mentions a similar sun-dial, in which a single cypress formed the dial.[1] Such a

MANNERS MAKYTH MAN

THE GARDEN. NEW-COLLEGE OXFORD FROM AN OLD ENGRAVING

Fig. 26.

garden, if it had been preserved, would have been beyond all price to us now. The ridicule with which such work is dismissed, the abuse lavished on it as artificial, is beside the mark. It is just this very artifice, this individuality, this human interest, that gives to the old formal garden its undying charm—the feeling that once there was a man or a woman who cared about

[1] *Théâtre d'Agriculture*, p. 531.

the garden enough to have it laid out in one
way more than another, and that they and
many generations since have taken pleasure in
its beauty and the fancy of its parterres.
Perhaps, when any tradition of art is formed
among us again, there will return this pleasure
and delight in those old ways which are the
better.

In the sixteenth century the flower-beds
were commonly square. The author of *The
Gardener's Labyrinth* advises that they should
be kept to such a size as that "the weeder's
handes may well reach into the middest of the
bed"; 12 feet by 6 is given as the size. Each
bed was to be raised about 1 foot above the
ground, but 2 feet in marshy ground. The
edges were to be cased in with stout planks
framed into square posts with finials at the
angles, with intermediate supports. Rea, in his
Flora, a hundred years later, advises beds and
the various parts of the frets for flowers to be
formed with planks in much the same way, but
the plank side was only to be 4 inches high.
Beds raised in this way about 18 inches above the
adjacent paths, and bordered with box-edgings,
can still be seen in the gardens at Versailles.
Besides the square flower-beds, a more intricate
form of bed, designed to fill up a square plot,
was much in use. This latter was called a
"knot." In the sixteenth century it seems to
have been usually formed with rosemary, hyssop,

and thyme. Five designs for knots are given
in *The Gardener's Labyrinth*, which were
to be formed entirely of hyssop or thyme.
In *The Countrie Housewife's Garden* (1617)
Lawson gives "divers new knots for gardens,"
viz. :—

Cinkfoyle	Lozenges
Flowers de luce	Grose-boowe
Trefoyle	Diamond
Frette	Ovall

Maze

All the flowers and herbs for these should,
he says, be planted by Michaeltide. The
borders were to be of "Roses, thorne, Lavender,
rosemaris, isop, sage, or such like," and filled
in with cowslips, primroses, and violets, "Daffy-
downdillies," "sweet Sissely," "go to bed at
noone," and all sweet flowers, and, chief of all,
with gillyflowers, the favourite flower of the
English Renaissance—"July flowers, commonly
called Gillyflowers,[1] or clove Jully flowers (I

---

[1] The name carnation gradually superseded the name gillyflower.
Worlidge refers to it as the vulgar name for gillyflower. "Carnation"
was at first used to describe one species, but came to be used for gillyflowers in general. Lawson's play upon words is pretty but improbable.
Gillyflower is possibly a corruption of *Guies Fleur*. A full account of
this flower and its various species will be found in Gerard's *Herbal*, chap.
172. Of clove Gillyflowers, Gerard says that these flowers were pro-
cured from Poland by a worshipful merchant of London, Master
Nicholas Lett, and given to him for his garden ; and that they had
never before "been seen or heard of in these countries," and further that
fresh varieties were being constantly introduced into England. He considered them not inferior to the Rose "in beauty, smell, and varietie."
Matthiolus, in his commentary on Dioscorides, p. 316, says that they
were called in France "Girophles," again probably a corruption of the
Latin name "Caryophyllus."

FIG. 27.—Knots, from Markham.

call them so because they flower in July);
they have the names of cloves of their scent.
I may well call them the king of flowers
(except the rose). Of all flowers (save the
Damaske rose) they are the most pleasant to
sight and smell." Markham says that "Of all
the best ornaments used in our English gardens, knots or mazes were the most ancient,
and at this day of most use among the vulgar,
the least respected with great ones." His list
of knots contains :—-

Straight line knots	Mixed knots
Diamond knots, single	Single Impleate
and double	of straight line
Single knots	Plain and mixed

Direct and circular

These knots were formed with a border of
box, lavender, or rosemary, 18 inches broad
at the bottom, and clipped so close and level
at the top as to form a table for the housewife to spread out clothes to dry on. Markham gives instructions how knots are to be
set out from designs on paper by subdividing
the square plot into a number of squares pro-
portional to those on the paper, and adds that
"You are to keep your level to a haire, for
if you faill in it you faill in your whole work."
He further describes two knots which anticipate
the *parterre de broderie*. In the first you set
out the lines of your design in germander or
hyssop, and fill in the parts with different

coloured earths and chalks, with camomile for
green. By this means you may represent
armorial bearings or anything else, and a very
poor affair it would probably have been. The
other knot sounds much more attractive. You
set out a plain knot, the larger the better. The
different "thrids" of the knot, as Markham
calls them, are to be planted with flowers of
one colour. Thus in one you will place
carnation gillyflowers, in another great white
gillyflowers, in another blood red, or hyacinths, or "dulippos." The knot will then
appear as if "made of divers coloured ribans."
The maze which appears in these descriptions
of knots was evidently only a figure for a
bed and not a labyrinth, such as the maze at
Hatfield or Hampton Court. Meager gives
some designs for knots and uses the term, but
he does not describe them, and his designs
are inferior to those of the beginning of the
seventeenth century. Knots seem to have
dropped out of use in the reign of Charles II.
The word occurs in London and Wise's translation of *The Retired Gard'ner*, and in James's
translation ; but the writers only deal with
parterres.

The parterre was introduced from France.
The old parterre corresponded to the English
knot, except that it was much more elaborate.
As early as 1600 Claude Mollet laid out parterres of embroidery for Henry IV. at the

Tuileries, Fontainebleau, and St. Germain-en-Laye. Seven engravings of these are given in Olivier de Serres's *Théâtre d'Agriculture et mesnage des Champs*, 1603. These were planted with flowers and grass edgings, and laid with coloured earths. The parterre was developed by Le Notre, and by the end of the seventeenth century a systematic classification was arrived at, which divided parterres into four main heads.[1] In James's translation of *The Theory and Practice of Gardening* they are given as follows :—" Parterres of embroidery, parterres of compartment, parterres after the English manner, and parterres of cut-work. There are also parterres of water, but at present they are quite out of use."

1. *Parterres de broderie* were designs similar to embroidered work, planted with edgings of box and filled up with different coloured earths, such as black earth composed of iron filings, or the scales beaten off the anvils, or powdered red tiles, or charcoal, or yellow sand. The foliage of the design was called "branchings," the flowers "flourishings."

2. *Parterres of compartment* are the same as the last, except that the design, instead of being single, is repeated both at the ends and the sides—that is to say, one quarter of the

---

[1] The term *parterre* was used generally to signify one specific plot or compartment of a garden, which formed a single design complete in itself.

whole parterre gives the design, and to complete the entire parterre this quarter has only
to be reversed and doubled, so that it is used up
four times.

3. *Parterres à l'Anglaise* were formed
simply with grass cut into various patterns and
bounded with box-edgings. Round the whole
parterre would run a sanded path, 2 to 3 feet
wide, and then a border of flowers to separate
it from the main walks. The terrace garden
overlooking the *pièce d'eau des Suisses*, at Versailles, is laid out with *parterres à l'Anglaise*,
but this parterre was never a success in France,
owing to the inferiority of the French to the
English turf.

4. Parterres of cut-work admitted neither
grass nor coloured earths, but every part of it
between the box-edgings was to be planted
entirely with flowers.

The paths between each part were to be
covered with yellow or white sand, and set
out at regular spaces with large Dutch jars
filled with flowers. London and Wise mention that it was once the custom to cover
the paths with potter's clay, well beaten, with
lees of oil. James specifies brick dust or tile
sherds powdered. In parterres of cut-work
all parts of the ground under the flowers and
within the box-edgings were to be covered
with fine sand.

Round these parterres were planted borders

from 4 to 6 feet wide, formed with a sharp
rising in the middle, "like a carp's back." [1]
These borders were either continuous all round
the parterre or cut into short lengths by cross
paths. They might be planted with flowers
or formed entirely of grass, with two small
sanded paths on either side, or entirely of sand
with a simple edging of box next the gravel
walk. In the two last cases they would be
set out with vases and flower-pots, or orange-
trees in cases, with yews in between, spaced
at regular intervals round the border. No
yews or shrubs were to be permitted to grow
more than 4 to 5 feet high, to avoid hiding
the parterre. The *plates-bandes isolées* of the
French were detached borders of flowers having
no relation to parterres. They were reserved
for the choicest flowers, and were enclosed
with borders of planks, such as those described
by Rea, painted green. Composite parterres
were formed by the combination of *parterres de
broderie* with cut-work and so on.

No instance of these parterres as at first
planted has survived, and it could not possibly
do so except in the case of the *parterre à
l'Anglaise*. Even the French author admits
that they are costly to lay out, and always lose
their form. On the whole the loss is not to
be regretted, for the designs shown in James's
translation, and particularly in Switzer's *Ichno-*

[1] *The Retired Gard'ner.*

graphia, are exceedingly absurd. The purpose
of a garden—to make the most of flowers and
velvety turf—was forgotten. The dignity of the
older formal garden was lost in these intricate
designs, which only led to a violent reaction in
favour of what was considered to be nature unadorned. Of all the parterres the *parterre à
l'Anglaise* was the least absurd, and the French-
men thought little of it. What is one to think
of a parterre laid out " with the mask-head of a
griffin having bats' wings formed by the sides of
grass-work, as the flourishes of the embroidery
form the nose, eyes, brows, moustaches, and
tuft upon the head of the mask " ? Much might
be done with simple parterres of grass and
flowers, but the elaborate system in fashion at
the beginning of the eighteenth century was a
pernicious abuse. It is significant that some of
the silliest of its features—such as the use of
coloured earths and broken tiles—have survived
in the practice of the landscape gardener.

Grass-work as an artistic quantity can hardly
be said to exist in landscape gardening. It is
there considered simply as so much background
to be broken up with shrubs and pampas grass
and irregular beds ; not as a means of effect in
itself, to be handled as a question of values,
both in regard to colour and amount. Lawn-
tennis and croquet have stopped some of the
worst faults of the landscapist by necessitating a
clear space of level lawn, and this large expanse

of uninterrupted grass has always been an
essential feature in formal garden design.

In the older garden, grass-work would include all artificial works intended to be turfed—
such as mounts, grass walks and banks, bowling-
greens, and theatres. The mount was a common
feature in English gardens as late as the middle
of the seventeenth century. They were the
natural result of the walled-in garden, in so far
as they provided the place from which the
owner could look abroad beyond his walls, and
were probably formed by the earth excavated for
the house. In the larger gardens there were
artificial mounts of considerable height raised at
some distance from the house, and usually
turfed and planted with trees. At the top
might be a banqueting-house. Kip's view of
Dunham Massie, in Cheshire, shows a circular
mount in four stages or terraces. Each stage
was fenced in with a pole-hedge, and at the top
was a garden-house with four gables. Leland
(*Itinerary*, p. 60) says that at Wresehall, in
Yorkshire, "in the orchardes were mountes,
opere topiarii writhen about with degrees like
turninges of cockell-shells, to cum to the top
without paine." It is possible that mounts of
this kind were suggested by a curious description of a medicinal garden given by Olivier de
Serres, and referred to by Markham. De Serres
gives two designs for these "montagnetes" (as
he calls them) or mounts. One was to be

circular in six stages, ascended by a continuous
walk like the Tower of Babel ; the other was to
be square in six stages, ascended by flights of
steps at the four angles. The stages were to be
15 feet wide—11 for the path and 4 for the
border of herbs. Each stage was to be 6 to 8
feet high, with retaining walls of masonry, and
the interior might be vaulted over as an inner
chamber for preserving the plants in winter.
The circular mount was 45 fathoms in diameter,
the square 50 fathoms by 50 ; but De Serres
suggests that these might be used on a very
much smaller scale. Worlidge mentions the
mount at Marlborough as the most considerable
in England at his time. This somewhat re-
sembles the circular mount of De Serres.
Mounts were usual in the smaller gardens as
well. The square mount in New College
garden still exists. The base of the mount
measures about 40 paces by 40 ; the height is
about 30 feet, but the original shape has been
lost, and it is now entirely overgrown with
trees and shrubs. There was a famous mount
in Wadham Gardens, circular in plan, with an
octagonal platform at the top reached by a
double flight of steps. In the centre of this
platform was a colossal figure of Atlas carrying
the globe. This mount stood in the centre of
the garden,[1] but their position appears to have

[1] The Wadham mount still exists, but the Atlas and all that made
ing have long since disappeared.

been arbitrary. The term was also used for the raised walk at the end of the garden.[1] Lawson mentions " mountes whence you may shoote a Buck " among the causes of delight in an orchard. " When you behold in divers corners of your orcharde mounts of stone or woode curiously wrought within and without, or of earth covered with fruit-trees ; Kentish cherry, damsones, plummes, etc., with staires of precious workmanship, and in some corner (or mo.) a true Dyall or clocke and some anticke workes, and especially silver-sounding musique, mixt instruments and voices gracing all the rest : how will you be rapt with delight ? Large walks, broad and long, close and open like the Tempe groves in Thessaly raised with gravel and sand, having seats and banks of camomile, all this delights the mind, and brings health to the body." The latest instance of a mount seems to have been the mount at New Park, in Surrey, which was laid out at the end of the seventeenth century, probably by London and Wise. The mount here was placed in the extreme upper right-hand corner to overlook the whole of the garden.

Grass walks have been already referred to in dealing with paths. Bowling-greens existed in almost every old English garden of any size. Borde refers to them, and Markham distinguishes between three sorts of bowling-grounds :

---

[1] See A Platform for Ponds, reproduced from Markham.

(1) The bowling-alley; (2) "open grounds of advantage"—that is, bowling-greens with a fall one way; (3) level bowling-greens. In *Country Contentments* (chap. viii.) he says, "Your flat bowles, being the best for close allies, your round byazed bowles for open grounds of advantage, and your round bowles like a ball for greene swarthes that are plaine and levell." A terrace or raised walk about 2 feet high often ran round the bowling-green, as at Cusworth, in Yorkshire. At Badminton a raised walk ran round two sides of the green, and at one end was a second raised alley for skittles. The shape of the green was usually square, and it seems to have been placed indifferently at the back or sides of the house. In later work the bowling-green was sometimes placed at a distance from the house, and laid out circular. At Cashiobury, laid out by Cook for Lord Essex, the bowling-green was placed at the end of a long avenue, and surrounded by a circular belt of fir-trees. At Penshurst the green was put out in the middle of a field. At Hampton Court the bowling-green is over half a mile from the palace. It is oval in plan and lies at the end of the Long Walk. This bowling-green is now planted over with trees. One of the pavilions remains; the other was destroyed in this century. Bowling-greens continued to be laid out in the eighteenth century. In Kip's view of

Knole in *Britannia Illustrata* no bowling-green
is shown ; but in Badeslade's view,[1] made about
twenty years later, a beautiful bowling-green is
shown on the south side of the house. This
was oval in plan, about 70 paces by 40, surrounded by a high clipped hedge with arbours
on the east and west sides, and openings on the
north and south. It was reached by a double
flight of steps from the lower parterres in front
of the house. From the fact that this is not
shown in Kip, it is probable that it was made
early in the eighteenth century. At Radley College, near Oxford, there is a long bowling-alley,
probably of the same date as the original house—
about the middle of the eighteenth century. At
Stratford-on-Avon there exists a square bowling-
green in excellent order, where, on the long
summer evenings, the game is still played with
much gravity and science. The object of a
bowling-green as a playing-ground was never
lost sight of in England. London and Wise
mention that a custom had been introduced of
planting tall trees round public bowling-greens
" rather to pleasure their customers than for
any advantage to their greens " ; but the green
itself was always kept open. From England
bowling-greens were introduced into France,
probably by Le Nôtre. The French called
them *boulingrins*, and quite lost sight of

---

[1] Badeslade's *Views of Noblemen's and Gentlemen's Seats in the County of Kent.*

their original purpose, for they made them of
all shapes and sizes, and as often as not put
a statue or a fountain in the middle of the
grass.   In the French system the *boulingrin*
only differed from the parterre in that the latter
was planted round with shrubs only, while
boulingrins were planted with trees — such
as elms, horse-chestnuts, and acacias (James).
In James's translation, *boulingrins* are defined
as "hollow sinkings and slopes of Turf, which
are practised either in the middle of very large
grass walks and green plots, or in a grove,
and sometimes in the middle of a parterre,
after 'the English mode.'   It is nothing but
a sinking that makes it a Bowling-green, together with the grass that covers it."   The
depth of these bowling-greens would be about
2 feet in the larger instances, about 18 inches
in the smaller.   They were divided into two
kinds—plain, consisting simply of grass-work,
with fine rolled paths between ; and composed,
which were laid out with trees, box, and palisades
of pleached work.   In the latter case fountains
or statues were sometimes placed in the middle
of the green.

The French further included in their classification of grass-work "ascents" of various
elaborate forms, which were generally subdivided into two heads—the *glacis* which was a
gentle slope, and the *talus* which was steep.
Besides the above varieties, theatres and banks of

different designs were formed in grass-work.
Grass theatres were more common on the continent than in England. The author of the
Théorie et Pratique talks of a " salle avec des
gradins servant d'amphithéâtre et de théâtre
pour jouer la comédie." In the gardens of the
Prince Bishops of Wurzburg there was a famous
amphitheatre formed of banks of turf, with clipped
hedges for scenery. This practice of designing
banks and recesses of grass-work might well be
revived on simpler lines, provided always that
geometrical forms are kept to—such as plain
curves or rectangular shapes—and that there is
none of that vague amorphous sloping in which
the landscape gardener delights. There is no
reason why a croquet lawn should not be laid
out on the lines of a bowling-green, with regular
sloped grass banks at the sides ; and at one end
a semicircular bay in grass might be formed,
or what the older writers used to call a cabinet
—that is, a regular recess with a well-trimmed
pole-hedge. There are great possibilities about
such a lawn properly handled—that is, if the
scale given by the dimensions of the croquet
ground itself is sedulously adhered to, and the
features introduced are kept sufficiently large
and simple. To make it a really valuable
part of the garden it is not enough to lay
out a sufficient expanse of grass, which loses
itself at the earliest opportunity in shrubs
and flower-beds. The lawn should be taken

as a definite problem, and designed as an integral part of the garden. And this applies to all grass-work. The mistake of the landscapist is that he considers grass only as a background, not as a very beautiful thing in itself. Grass-work ought to be designed with reference to its own particular beauty. The turf of an English garden is probably the most perfect in the world, certainly it is far more beautiful than any to be found on the continent, and even the French admitted this two hundred years ago. It is wilfully throwing away a most valuable means of delight to treat grass-work as a mere affair of hap-hazard convenience. Here, perhaps, most of all, in order to get out of grass-work its full possibility of beauty, is necessary that decent order and restraint, that fine sobriety of taste that once reigned paramount over all the arts of design in England.

THE GARDEN : CANONS ASHBY : NORTHAMPTONSHIRE

CHAPTER VII

FISH-PONDS, PLEACHING, ARBOURS, GALLERIES, HEDGES, PALISADES, GROVES

THE double purpose of a garden—for use and pleasure—has been forgotten in landscape gardening. You either get a kitchen garden useful but ugly, or a pleasure garden not useful, and only redeemed from ugliness by the flowers themselves. The charm of the older garden is in the combination of the two, or rather the way in which grounds and water laid out, not solely for their beauty, were made beautiful by their reasonable order. The old fish-pond with its regular grass banks is a charming thing in itself, yet this was at first as much a matter of necessity as the poultry-house or the dove-cote. Here lived the lazy carp, the pike, the perch, the bream, the tench, and other fish that might

be wanted for the table. A slow stream of
running water kept the fish-pond fresh, and at
one end was formed a "stew," or small tank,
to keep the fish that were netted. Markham
describes the formation of a fish-pond in some
detail (*Cheape and Good Husbandrie*, book ii.,
London 1638). First drain your ground and
bring all the water to one head or main reservoir. From this you form your canal to supply
the pond. The sides of the canal are to be
formed with piles, 6 feet long and 6 inches
square, of oak, ash, or elm, to be driven in in
rows and the earth well rammed behind them.
You then form the sides of your pond with
sloping banks covered with large sods of plot
grass laid close and pinned down with small
stakes. "On one side you are to stake down
Bavens or faggots of brushwood for the fish to
spawn in, and some sods piled up for the
comfort of the eels, and if you stick sharp
stakes slantwise by every side of the pond that
will keep thieves from robbing them." To
explain his advice, Markham gives "a platform
for ponds" (reproduced in the text), which
shows a perfectly symmetrical arrangement of
a square with a triangular extension on the
entrance side. The walks between the canals
and ponds were to be planted with willows or
fruit-trees. Markham also describes another
method of dealing with marshy ground, by
which an orchard might be combined with a

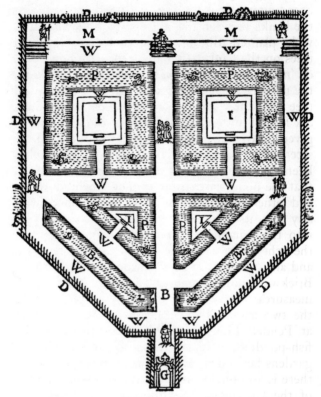

FIG. 28.—From Markham's *Cheape and Good Husbandrie.*

G. The Gate.	P. The Ponds.
D. The Ditch and quickset hedge.	I. The Peniles.
W. The Walkes.	M. The Mount.
B. The Bridge. | Br. The Brooke.	S. The Springhead.

The walkes about the pond may be planted with fruit-trees or willows.

fish-pond. You dig a series of ditches 16 feet broad and 9 deep, 12 feet apart in parallel rows, the banks between to be 7 feet high and 12 feet wide, planted with osier at the sides and fruit-trees on the banks—"Thus you will get a sort of maze and pleasant fish-ponds." Perhaps the gardens at Theobalds described by Hentzner (see chap. ii.) were laid out in this manner. Six feet of water and 2 feet for the banks are given by Markham as maximum depths. The size would be arbitrary. Lawson, who had a keener eye for beauty than Markham, advises that the pond should be large enough for swans and other water birds. The fish-pond gradu-ally lost its practical character and developed into the ornamental water ; it became part of the scheme of the garden design, grass banks and all. There is a good instance of this in the Brickwall gardens, where the fish-pond, which measures 32 paces by 12 wide, occupies one of the two main plots. There is another instance at Pendell House, near Bletchingley, where the fish-pond divides the lawn from the flower gardens beyond. At Sydenham, in Devonshire, there is an oblong piece of water in the middle of the lawn with a circular basin for a fountain in the centre. The grass banks required a good deal of attention to keep them trim, and this led to the substitution of brick or stone sides instead of grass in more important work ; and when the influence of Le Nôtre extended

THE OLD GARDENS AT BRICKWALL, NEAR NORTHIAM : SUSSEX

Fig. 29.

to England, the fish-pond as a fish-pond disappeared in the vast sheets of water which
formed an essential feature in his system of
design. Great canals and basins, as at Wrest,
in Bedfordshire, took its place, and the transition from this to the artificial lakes of the

THE FISHPOND : WREST : BEDFORDSHIRE

Fig. 30.

landscape gardener was easy. The great canal
at Wrest measures about 250 paces by 50, with
transepts at the north end and a large pavilion
at the south. There is also at Wrest a pond
called "the Ladies' Canal," with grass banks
measuring about 90 paces by 40. This is
surrounded by a broad grass verge and yew-
hedges 20 feet high, with a statue at the west

end. The fish-pond at Penshurst measures about 35 paces by 21.0; it has brick side walls, a grass verge 10.9 wide, and yew-hedges 7.6 high on all four sides. The water pieces at Melbourne are rather elaborate, one, with a fountain in the centre, is laid out as an oblong with circular bays on the sides. The main piece is formed by an oblong 72 paces by 43, with a half-quatrefoil extension on the farther side. This is surrounded by grass verges on either side of a gravel path, and yew-hedges with recesses for seats and statues. Opposite the centre, on the farther side, is the famous wrought-iron garden-house. The Long Canal at Hampton Court, measuring 150 feet by 3.500, and formed in the reign of Charles II., is probably the largest instance of the kind in England.

"Pleaching" is probably the best abused of the many iniquities of the formal garden. The man of "nature" says it is unnatural, and it gives an occasion for cheap ridicule too obvious to be resisted. But those who have a weakness for the vicious old practice are in good company. The Romans used to do all sorts of things in pleaching, and so did everybody else down to the end of the seventeenth century and later. The word "pleach" means the trimming of the small boughs and foliage of trees or bushes to bring them to a regular shape, and, of course, only certain species will submit to this treatment—such as lime, horn-beam, yew, box, holly, white-thorn, and privet, kinds that are " humble and tonsile," as an old writer calls them.   Pleaching must be dis-tinguished from another old word still in use, " plashing," which refers to the half-cutting of the larger branches and bending them down to form a hedge.   Markham explains " plashing " to be " a half-cutting or dividing of the quicke growth almost to the outward barke, and then laying it orderly in a sloape manner, as you see a cunning hedger lay a dead hedge, and then with the smaller and more plyant branches to wreathe and bind in the tops."   Pleaching was employed to form mazes, arbours or bowers, green walks, colonnades, and hedgerows, besides the infinite variety of cut-work in yew and box.

Mazes were formed all through the seven-teenth century.   The one at Hatfield is a perfect instance.   The maze at Hampton Court is another familiar example.   This appears to have been planted in the time of William III., and it is not probable that many were laid out after that date.   The bower or green arbour existed in the mediæval garden, but probably in a somewhat artless form.   The earliest account of arbours is found in *The Gardener's Labyrinth*; the writer classifies arbours as upright or winding.   The upright arbour was simply a lean-to, the winding or arch arbour an independent arbour standing by itself.   At the end of the seventeenth century

a further distinction was made between bowers
and arbours; a bower was always long and
arched, an arbour was either round or square,
domed over at the top. The older arbours were
formed with poles of juniper or willow framed
square and bound with osiers, and were covered
with roses trimmed and trained to the framing,
or with jessamine, rosemary, juniper, or cypress
(Markham); or with bryony, cucumber and
gourd. "Mountaine" adds that as arbours of
roses required a great deal of attention "the most
number in England plant vines for the lesser
travaile to nurse and spread over the upright
and square Herbers, framed with quarters and
poles reaching abreadth." These arbours fell
into disuse for four excellent reasons, given by
Worlidge : "(1) they quickly fall out of repair ;
(2) the seats are damp; (3) the rain drips
longer here than anywhere else ; (4) they are
draughty, and on a hot day it is pleasanter to sit
under a lime-tree than to be hoodwinked in an
arbour." Besides the arbours there were the
long covered walks and galleries, arched over at
the top, with a solid hedge on the outer side,
and openings or "windows properly made towards the garden, wherebye they might the more
fully view and have delight of the whole beauty
of the garden." Bacon contemplated a green
gallery such as this to run round the sides of his
outer garden. There were some remarkable
instances in the old gardens at Wilton. The

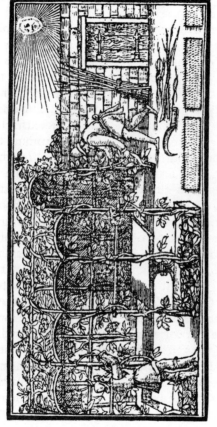

FIG. 31.—From *The Gardener's Labyrinth*.

views published by Isaac de Caux show long
green galleries arched over with pavilions at the
ends and in the centre ; and some less elaborate
galleries are shown in Logan's views of Pembroke, Oxford. The prints reproduced from
The Gardener's Labyrinth and *The Hortus
Floridus* of Crispin de Pass show their general
character. The long yew walk at Melbourne
is really a green gallery without the openings.
It was planted early in the eighteenth century.
Its length from the top to the fountain is 120
paces, its width inside 12 feet. The yew has
grown into an impenetrable vault of branches
overhead, so thick that it is proof against an
ordinary shower of rain. The green gallery was
not an importation of the sixteenth century, but
a direct survival of the mediæval garden. In
" The Romance of the Rose " there are several
beautiful illustrations of these green galleries,
formed of light poles framed square, as described
in *The Gardener's Labyrinth*, and overgrown with
roses, red and white. They continued in use
till the end of the seventeenth century, when,
as was the case with nearly all that was beautiful
in the formal garden, they were elaborated out
of all reason, and only continued in use in quiet
country gardens where the master loved his
garden, and liked the old ways better than the
new. In *The Retired Gard'ner*, by London and
Wise, full directions are given for the information
of green galleries and porticoes and colonnades of

Fig. 32.—Garden, from Crispin de Pass.

cut-work. The galleries should be 8 to 10
feet broad and 12 or 15 feet high, the outer
side solid, the inner side open as a gallery,
with pillars formed by the trunks of the trees,
set 4 feet apart, with a low hedge 3 feet high
between each trunk. These were generally
formed of lime or hornbeam. "Natural
arbours" as opposed to arbours of trellis-work
were formed of elm, lime, and hornbeam in the
same way. A rough framework of wood or
iron seems to have been used in the first instance
to start the trees on the required lines. After
they were fairly set, the trees were brought into
shape by wreathing the boughs together and
constant clipping. There is a good example of
a pleached alley at Drayton House, Northants,
"just as Sir John Germain brought it from
Holland," as Horace Walpole wrote in 1763.

Hedges, of course, could only be formed by
pleaching. The older gardeners preferred a
close-grown hedge, white-thorn or privet, to any
other form of fencing round a garden. It was
pleasant to look on, and more difficult to get
over than any wall. *The Gardener's Labyrinth*
says "the most commendable enclosure for
every garden plot is a quick-set hedge, made
with Brambles and white-thorn." Lawson
advises a double ditch and a hedge of thorn,
though "it will hardly availe you to make any
fence for your orchard, if you be a niggard of
your fruite." These hedges were planted in two

or three rows, kept behind shelter for three or
four years, and clipped at every possible oppor-

THE YEW WALK : MELBOURNE DERBYSHIRE

FIG. 33.

tunity ; about 6 or 7 feet was a usual height.
Worlidge, who was nothing if not practical,

again classifies the reasons for preferring white-thorn for hedges : (1) it grows quickest, and is most easily trimmed ; (2) it is stronger and most durable ; (3) it is of a delicate colour ; (4) it puts out its leaves the earliest in spring. Markham allows five to seven years for a quick-

FIG. 34.—Hedge, from Markham's *Country Farm*.

set of white-thorn. In *The Country Farm* he gives some designs for the shaping of hedges. The quarters of his garden are to be fenced with "fine curious hedges made battlement-wise in sundrie forms according to invention, or carrying the proportions of Pyllasters, flowers, shapes of beasts, birds, creeping things, shippes, trees and such-like." A framework is to be formed of square framing bound with osiers and wire. At the foot of this in the spring or autumn "you shall set white - thorn, eglantine, and sweet-briar mixt together, and as they shall shoot and grow up, so you shall wind and pleach them within the lattice-work, making them grow and cover the same," and always trimming to the shape required. In about two or three years, he says, you will get an excellent, strong hedge. Evelyn in his *Sylva* (Hawthorn) criticises Markham's directions as to plashing, and gives very full particulars as to the proper method of forming a quick-set hedge. In Herefordshire he notices that a crab-tree stock was invariably planted every 20 feet apart in the quick-set. For many years after Markham wrote the custom of cutting the tops of hedges into fanciful shapes continued in use. There is a good example in yew at Cleeve Prior manor-house, in Warwickshire, and the doves at Risley, mentioned before. Evelyn claims that he was the first to bring yew into fashion, not only for hedges, but also as "a succedaneum to cypress, whether in hedges or pyramids, cones, spires, bowls, or what other shapes." Buttresses and ramps, little square towers, finials of various forms, archways and canopies were cut in yew as late as the beginning of this century in out-of-the-way places and in the smaller gardens. The well-known instances at Arley, in Cheshire, and Penshurst are not more than thirty-five years old. Besides white-thorn, privet, and yew, the sweet-briar, pyracantha, and holly were commonly used for hedges. Holly was the special favourite of Evelyn, because of its power of defence and the sheen of its leaves. At Sayes Court he had a holly-hedge 400 feet long, 9 feet high, and 5 feet thick. This hedge was his special pride till Peter the Great came to live at Deptford, and formed a habit of amusing himself after his labours in shipbuilding by charging the hedge in a wheel-barrow. Evelyn says he had seen hedges of holly 20 feet high "kept upright, and the gilded sort budded low, and in two or three places one above another, shorn and fashioned into columns and pilasters, architectonically shaped and at due distance, than which nothing can possibly be more pleasant, the berry adorning the intercolumniations with scarlet festoons and encarpa." The worst possible bush for a hedge is the laurel. It starts with great promise, and everything goes well for two or three years, after which it gets thin and straggly underneath, and becomes shabbier and shabbier every year. The only chance with it is to cut it and clip it without remorse. In some old-fashioned gardens, where fruit-trees and flowers are allowed to grow together, beautiful hedges are formed by apple-trees grown as espaliers.[1]

---

[1] In Mr. Robinson's *Parks and Gardens of Paris* there is a useful description of the French methods of forming trellis-hedges of pear and apple and other fruit trees.

Palisades or pole-hedges were high hedges formed of trees—such as lime, elm, or horn-beam. These were usually of great length and height, and the point to be aimed at was to keep them entirely smooth and even, making, as it were, a great wall of green tapestry, " all the beauty of which consists in being well filled up from the very bottom, of no great thickness, and handsomely clipped on both sides as per-pendicularly as possible." Where the palisades had to be very high the stems of the trees were kept bare of branches, and the intervals up to the level of the lowest branch planted with yew or box trimmed to form a solid screen. At Brickwall there is a palisade of lime-trees along one side of the garden. The branches are trained and trimmed to form a continuous curtain, starting about 10 feet from the ground, and behind the trees is an old red-brick wall up to the level of the boughs. A palisade of this sort is delightful in colour, and easily kept in shape if properly pleached ; and in this respect it is more satisfactory than very great walls of yew, which are apt to lose their symmetry and become obese and corpulent as soon as they have reached maturity. Evelyn particularly commends the hornbeam. " Being planted in small fosses or trenches, at half-a-foot interval and in the single row, it makes the noblest and stateliest hedge for long walks in gardens or parks . . . because it grows tall and so sturdy as not to be wronged by the winds ; besides it will furnish to the very foot of the stem, and flourishes with a glossy and polished verdure, which is exceedingly delightful." He mentions the long walk of the Luxembourg and "the close walk with that perplext canopy which lately covered the seat in his Majesty's garden at Hampton Court," and the hedges at New Park, as instances of hornbeam hedges. At the end of the seventeenth century much money was spent in forming palisades of different architectural forms. Twenty thousand crowns were spent in work of this sort at the gardens of the Hôtel de Condé. London and Wise are minute in their directions. The arcades were to be formed of elm, lime, or hornbeam—elm for preference. The elms were to be planted in a straight line 8 to 10 feet apart. Elms about 6 feet high and " as thick as your arm " (the two dimensions do not quite agree) were to be used. In the second year after planting you began to form the columns by selecting the likeliest boughs and binding them with osiers to a wooden post, and cutting off the rest. The arches were formed by binding hoops of wood to the posts and training the boughs to these as before. In the spandrels will be left a tuft of foliage, which you trim to the shape of an apple or any other form you please. Each column will be about 16 feet high—6 feet of plain stem, and 10 feet for the column itself formed of the boughs and foliage. James's translation gives twice the breadth as the right proportion for the height of the arches, and adds that a hedge breast-high should be made between the columns, and niches and recesses for statues and seats formed in the palisade. The palisade was to be double—that is, planted in two rows with a grass walk in between, and between each column there was to be a border set with double gillyflowers, roses, or Indian pinks ; on the outer side there was to be a dwarf hedge of hornbeam 18 inches high. London and Wise describe other varieties of pleached work which sound suspicious. For instance, along the sides of walks or the borders of parterres elms might be planted and trimmed into round-headed standards, the stem quite bare for 6 feet or so from the ground, and the branches clipped into balls of foliage ; or hornbeam might be planted round the elm, and cut low to form the base, or balls of rose-trees formed between the standards. These could only look well if used with delicate tact and the greatest reticence ; unfortunately these were just the qualities in which the gardeners of the early eighteenth century were wanting. But a lilac walk formed with standards 12 feet apart, with stems 10 feet high, and a palisade of hornbeam in between, sounds better ; and London and Wise mention a hedge of pyracantha to go round a narrow place enclosed with walls, which in colour and form might be quite beautiful. At regular intervals cypress-trees were to be planted, with stems kept bare for 8 or 10 feet, and the spaces between were to be filled up with a hedge of pyracantha cut close against the wall.

At the end of the seventeenth century the laying out of groves was regularly included in garden design. In the earlier Renaissance garden little was done in this direction except in the way of mazes; a space outside the garden was often reserved for a wilderness such as Bacon describes, in which design was purposely abandoned. But the growing tendency was to reduce the garden to a system, till it reached its climax in the school of Le Nôtre, and the *bosquet* or grove of regular form took the place of the wilderness. Chapter vi. of *The Theory and Practice of Gardening* is entirely devoted to "woods and groves." " Their most usual forms are the star, the direct cross, the Saint Andrew's Cross, and goose-foot.[1] They nevertheless admit of the following designs, as cloisters, quincunxes, Bowling-greens, Halls, cabinets, circular and square compartments, halls for comedy, covered halls, natural and artificial arbours, fountains, isles, cascades, water galleries, green galleries, etc." These groves were to be laid out with

---

[1] The "goose-foot," *patte-d'oie*, consisted of three avenues radiating from a small semicircle. The three great avenues at Hampton Court, with the semicircular garden, form a goose-foot.

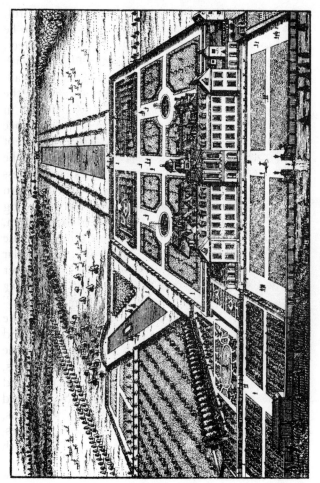

FIG. 35.—Wrest, from Kip.

walks from 12 to 24 feet wide, separated from
the trees by palisades. The trees in these
groves were not supposed to exceed 40 feet in
height or thereabouts, and they might either
have underwood or not, as desired. Where
there was no underwood, trees—such as limes,
elms, or horse-chestnuts—were to be planted in
regular lines at right angles to each other, the
stems kept bare for 10 feet and the trees
set out about 15 feet apart. The ground
underneath was either fine gravelled, or laid
with grass. In the latter case a circle about
4 feet across, without grass, was to be left
round each tree. There are good examples of
groves laid out to a regular design at Wrest
and Melbourne, but the best instances of this
sort of work are to be found in France. In
many towns and villages on the banks of the
Seine between Paris and Rouen, and elsewhere
in France, there are charming groves of
lime-trees, symmetrically planted and regularly
clipped. The groves at Versailles are still
much as Le Nôtre left them. The great
walks of lime-trees, close trimmed for 20 feet
or more, and the halls cleared in the groves
and set out with statues are very beautiful
on a sunny day ; but the rest of the work
is dull, and there can be no doubt that this
kind of work does require great space and
great expense to be seen to perfection. In *The
Theory and Practice of Gardening* forty-four

different designs are given for the largest groves. Some are simple enough, but most of them are absurdly elaborate, more particularly a design of a labyrinth (like a Catherine wheel) with cabinets and fountains, which it would be quite impossible to carry out. Over-elaboration, incapacity for self-suppression, these were the vices which wrecked the formal garden, and opened the way for every kind of imposture. With evident complacency, London and Wise remarked that it is certain "the Industry of Gard'ners was never equal to what it is now." It is also certain that this misapplied industry was foredoomed to failure, and that the disappearance of the formal garden was its inevitable result.

THE WATER PAVILION: WREST: BEDFORDSHIRE

CHAPTER VIII

Garden Architecture

BRIDGES, GATEHOUSES, GATEWAYS, GATES, WALLS, BALUSTRADES, STAIRS

Since the disappearance of the formal garden, the necessity of scholarly design for garden buildings has been forgotten, and the result is seen in buildings and details, which are not simple and childlike, but wholly pretentious and bad. This is not solely due to the enterprise of the landscape gardener. The fault lies also with his employer, who, perhaps,

prefers the cast-iron finials and meagre woodwork of his conservatory, and possibly takes
pleasure in the grotesque impossibilities of
his rustic summer-house, but who on any
showing, has not realised that art has to be
taken as a whole, that it must penetrate everywhere, that it is not enough to have a well-
designed house, if everything inside it is vulgar ;
or a house complete, with a meaningless garden ;
or a fair house and garden, with no thought
given to its walls and gateways. Till the end
of the eighteenth century a tradition of good
taste existed in England—a tradition not con-
fined to any one class, but shown not less in the
sampler of the village school than in the architecture of the great lord's house. It might be
said to have lingered on into this century in
sleepy country towns. Behind the lawyer's
house, with its white sash-windows and delicate
brick work, there may still survive some delightful garden bright with old-fashioned flowers
against the red-brick wall, and a broad stretch
of velvety turf set off by ample paths of gravel,
and at one corner, perhaps, a dainty summer-
house of brick, with marble floor and panelled
sides ; and all so quiet and sober, stamped with
a refinement which was once traditional, but
now seems a special gift of heaven.

It would be impossible here to give more
than a general sketch of the details of garden
architecture. The field is a wide one, and

could only be fully handled in relation to the art
of the time. Such subjects as bridges and gatehouses, for instance, would take their place in a
specific treatise on architecture. Where the house,
as was often the case, was surrounded by water,
the enclosure was reached by a bridge, sometimes
of wood, more often of brick or stone. There
is only one point to be noticed here in regard to
these bridges, and that is, that as much thought
and architectural knowledge were devoted to
their details as were spent on those of the house.
No such ragged and rickety structure as "the
rustic bridge" would have been tolerated in the
formal garden. The bridge at Clare (College),
Cambridge, designed by a builder-architect, is a
simple and very beautiful example, and perhaps
there is no better instance in the whole range of
garden architecture in England which shows
more clearly the absolute interdependence of
architecture and garden design. On the other
hand these bridges were sometimes unnecessarily
sumptuous. The well-known example at Blenheim is a standing monument of Vanbrugh's
megalomania. The Palladian bridge at Wilton
is a fine piece of academical design, but it is
rather unreasonable in England. When the
landscapists were destroying the formal garden
they preserved some of its worst features, among
them the Palladian bridge, which was repeated
literally both at Stowe and Prior Park.

The gatehouse in the sixteenth century

usually formed part of the block of house buildings, and was marked by rising one storey above
the rest.   The gateway of a college quadrangle
is a familiar instance.   When the fore court

THE PALLADIAN BRIDGE : WILTON : WILTSHIRE :

Fig. 36.

developed into a well-defined courtyard the
gateway was detached from the house, but still
continued to be a building of two or more
storeys, with wing walls to the right and left
joining the side walls of the court.   Charlcote,
in Warwickshire, and Burton Agnes, near

Bridlington, in Yorkshire, are good examples in brick and stone. At Lanhydrock, in Cornwall, there is a curious two-storey gatehouse in stone, standing at the end of a fine avenue of syca-mores, 37 paces wide, with counter avenues of beeches 16 paces wide. Another remarkable gatehouse is that of Westwood, in Worcester-shire, shown in Kip's views. This is probably Elizabethan. The gateway is set back between two projecting bays with stone gables. The wall between is of brick, the upper part of open strapwork in stone. Over the centre of the building rises a square stage of oak framing, slated, for a clock or bell. In Atkyns's *Glou-cestershire* (p. 340) a view is given of Shipton Moyne, showing a gatehouse flanked with turrets, and a room over the arch, apparently reached by steps from a raised terrace running round the fore court. There is a somewhat similar instance at Bolsover Castle. The gate-way stands in a polygonal wall of sufficient thickness to admit of a walk along the top all round the court, this walk being reached from a small door from the first floor of the keep. The gateway of Hardwick House, with its open strapwork, is a very ugly instance of a gate-house to the fore court in one storey. The gateway was sometimes flanked on either hand by small one-storey buildings for a porter's lodge, as at Ribston, in Yorkshire ; or the gateway was simply an archway in the courtyard wall, with a cornice and gable or pediment over. There is a curious instance at Bradshaw Hall, in Derbyshire, 1620. With the introduction of long avenues a further change was made. The gatehouse in front of the house interfered with the view of the façade. The fore court was accordingly enclosed with wrought-iron railings on a low wall, and elaborate entrance gates between piers of masonry or brickwork, and the gatehouse was shifted to the other end of the avenue. There are many instances of these gatehouses or lodges dating from the eighteenth century. In all cases their details follow those of the architecture of the house. The later instances of the eighteenth century degenerated into various versions of little Greek temples, rather ridiculous to look at, and quite unsuitable for the lodge-keepers to live in. The best position for the gatehouse would be high level ground overlooking the park. The one place where it should never stand is on the side of a hill, for the simple reason that while the gates are being opened carts and carriages have to stand on a slope. There is an instance of this at Prior Park, near Bath.

The main entrance gateway was usually placed in the centre of the fore court, opposite the front door, though this position was varied to suit particular cases. In smaller houses the gateway stood at the end of a broad flagged path leading up to the house, and visitors had to alight in the road outside. These gateways were sometimes arched, and sometimes consisted simply of stone or brick piers. There is a good instance in the town of Wilton of a small gateway with a circular arch, flanked by pilasters, with a circular pediment over and stone brackets at the sides. On either side of the gateway are wing walls completing the semicircle. There are instances at Bradford-on-Avon and many other places. They are usually quiet and simple in detail and excellently built, for the masonry of the eighteenth century is probably the best that ever was done in England. The piers on either side of the gates show every variety of design. The most familiar instance is the square pier of brick or stone with moulded base and top, and a great stone cannon-ball. These seem to have come into use in the latter part of the seventeenth century, and to have lasted to the beginning of this. There are many instances in London. Those at Ashburnham House are well known. There is a late but very well-designed example (about 1780) in the Euston Road, at the entrance to Maple's timber-yard. At Eyam Hall, Derbyshire, the piers are of stone, divided by bands into three carved panels. At Risley the piers are of brick for a height of 8 feet 6 inches; above this is a stone pedestal 2 feet 9 inches high, with cannon-ball finials. The piers are 9 feet apart, and the wing walls with the gate form half an

ellipse 38.0 long.   There are fine examples at
Swarkestone, in Derbyshire, and Mapperton,
in Somersetshire.   Besides the cannon-balls,
urns of all sorts were placed on the top of
the piers, as at Okeover, in Staffordshire, and
the great brick piers in Lincoln's Inn Fields,
attributed to Inigo Jones; or obelisks, as at

EYAM : DERBYSHIRE :

Fig. 37.

Canons Ashby and Hardwick; or eagles, as
in the Gray's Inn gardens; or heraldic beasts
or devices, as at Montacute and Canons Ashby;
or trophies of arms, as in the gateway at
Hampton Court.   The piers themselves were
varied indefinitely.   Those at Groombridge
Place have an additional pier on the outer side,
with a niche for a seat.   At Scalby, near Scar-
borough, the piers consist of two small towers,

about 3 feet in diameter, with cornices and stone domed roof. The most difficult of all to design satisfactorily is the plain pier and cannon-ball.

Besides the main gateway, there were the gate-

GATE PIERS: CANONS ASHBY: NORTHANTS

FIG. 38.

ways in garden-walls, leading from the fruit to the flower garden, or from one part of the garden to another, or from the paddock to the garden. Markham says " the false gate (otherwise called the back or field-gate) in that side toward your medow, made for your going in

or out alone, shall be set out and garnished
with two chevrons, set upon one maine timber
and no more, and foure
or five battlements." At
Coley Hall, near Halifax,
there is a garden gateway
of stone not unlike Mark-
ham's description. It is
dated 1649, and there are
good seventeenth-century
examples at Orwalle, in
North Hants, and Stibb-
ington Hall, in Hunting-

Fɪɢ. 39.

donshire. The stepped battlement form was
commonly used for brick and stone gateways;
there is a curious seventeenth-century example

Fɪɢ. 40.

on the terrace at Risley. The gateway stands
at the head of a flight of steps leading to the
terrace. In the centre is a square-headed door

flanked by niches on both sides, and above is a blank piece of wall with a stepped gable, with stepped side walls descending to the lower walk. These walls draw in as they approach the centre wall. The gateway to the churchyard at Martock (1627) is another simple instance of a stone gateway at the head of a flight of steps. The gateway at Tissington, in Derbyshire, is rather unusual ; it appears to date from the middle of the seventeenth century. In the wall to the side terrace at Penshurst there is a good brick gateway of about the same date or a little earlier.

The gates themselves were usually of wrought iron of every degree of elaboration, from the plain bar and rail to such intricate work as Tijou's splendid gates for Hampton Court. The hundred years, from the Restoration onward, is the golden age of smith's work in England. Tijou's example gave the craft an impetus in an entirely new direction ; wrought-iron gates of beautiful design and admirable workmanship were turned out in every part of the country, and it is not easy to account for the strong family resemblance between instances as far apart as Sydenham, in Devonshire, Chiddingstone, in Kent, or the Chelsea gates, the delicate work at Oxford or Cambridge, and the various examples scattered about in Derbyshire and the north. The gates and railings to New College Gardens and the Trinity gates at Oxford

GARDEN GATE: TISSINGTON: DERBY.

Fig. 41.

are characteristic instances of eighteenth-century work. It appears, from the diary of Celia Fiennes, that these gates were usually painted blue and gold. The worst of it is that about the time that the ironwork is supposed to want repainting, the blue reaches the very perfection of its colour. It has taken its place in nature, and this is the difficulty about all external painting. It is no use starting with delicate shades of green and blue ; the colour flies and a cold uninteresting gray is left. It is best to start with a good strong coat of honest green, and leave it to the sun and rain to bring about the refinements of colour seen in old painted work. This beautiful art of wrought-iron work might well be employed again more freely in garden gates and grilles. It is very unobtrusive, and it is pleasant to come upon its subtle workmanship, set in the rough surface of the garden-wall. Like many other handicrafts, it has gone down before the cry for cheapness. People supposed that they got the sort of thing in cast-iron work at a tenth of the price, and they are quite satisfied with "the sort of thing," the *à peu près*, provided it is cheap, forgetting first that there is no pleasure in a mechanical repetition even if the original is good, and secondly, that cast iron is a perfectly unsuitable material for gates. Cast iron is brittle and heavy ; it is well enough for stationary work, but it is apt to fly at a sudden jar, and to gain the necessary strength it must be made clumsy and awkward. A wrought-iron gate can be made as light as you please, and instead of being an inert mass, it has a tough vitality of its own. The craft as usual lingered longest in the country. In the villages of Somerset and Devonshire there are still to be seen pretty little wrought-iron gates to the cottage gardens, not yet supplanted by the odious castings of the hardware dealer.

The garden-walls should be of brick or stone, brick for preference, because it is better adapted for nailing fruit-trees, and retains the heat better than stone, and the creepers cling to it more readily. Rea gives 9 feet as the proper height for the outer wall of the garden, and 5 or 6 feet for cross-walls. Markham says that "james or offshoots" should be built 12 or 14 feet apart as buttresses to reduce the amount of brickwork and shelter the fruit. Worlidge, who repeats this advice, adds that pieces of wood should be built in, or iron hooks to project about 3 or 4 inches from the wall, to carry wooden rails to which the fruit-trees can be fastened. There is a good instance of plain walling at Hampton Court beside the Long Walk. The offsets are 18 inches wide, composed of blocks of stone alternating with five courses of brickwork ; a moulded stone coping covers the top, the section of which is changed when it returns round the offsets. The copings can be of brick on edge with tile creasings, or of stone, or of brick

variously arranged. The garden-walls of Ham
House have a rather elaborate brick coping.
The buttresses came to be treated as piers with
moulded cornices and finial balls or urns, and
the wall space between was treated variously,
either kept low with an iron grille between the
piers, as was commonly done at the end of
walks or where any particular view was desired ;
or the wall and its coping was shaped as a curve
rising to the piers on either side. At Pendell
House the wall along the raised walk at the end
of the garden is built with great flat curves
between the piers some 35 feet apart.
Instead of buttresses, the wall was sometimes
built on a serpentine line, as at Stubbers,
in Essex. By means of the resistance of the
curves on plan, a thin wall would stand without
buttresses ; but the effect is not pleasant, and
a good deal of ground is wasted. A thin wall
in the garden looks poor ; the old garden-walls
were seldom less than 18 inches thick, and
some were thick enough to contain bee-hives and
peacock-hutches. At Packwood House, in
Warwickshire, on the south side of the terrace-
wall there are thirty small niches for bee-hives,
two and two between the piers ; and at Riddles-
den, in Yorkshire, there still exist the cells for
peacocks, built into the thickness of the garden-
wall. There are four of these, two above and
two below, with shelves for nesting. The lower
pair have hooks for doors, which are gone, the

upper pair have shaped stone heads. The
gardens of Edzell Castle have a remarkable
stone wall, divided into bays, 10 to 11 feet
wide, by engaged shafts rising up into a string
course. These bays have alternately a single
recess 3 feet by 2.6, and three rows of smaller
recesses about 1.4 inches square arranged
chequer-wise—all the recesses appear to have
been used for planting flowers in them. Above
the single recesses there are bas-reliefs representing emblematical figures ; above the smaller
ones three stars. Over the centre of each bay is
a niche with a circular pediment.

The retaining walls under terraces were often
treated in the same way ; niches for statues,
recesses for seats, as at Kilworthy, in Devon,
grottoes, and toolhouses were often built in
below the terrace level. There is a cellar of
this description under one of the terraces at
Penshurst. Worlidge describes a grotto to be
made under a terrace. It was to be arched over
with stone or brick, or the roof might be of
stone supported by pillars of marble. The
sides were to be of stone and the floors of
marble. If there were any secret rooms to
the grotto, they might be made with "tables"
of stone or marble. He mentions a grotto at
Wilton as famous in his time. In stone
countries the retaining walls were of stone ;
elsewhere they were usually of brick with stone
balustrades and flights of steps. The commonest

form of balustrade, and on the whole the most
satisfactory, consisted of stone balusters with
moulded plinths and copings divided up by solid
piers. There is a good simple instance at
Woolley Green, near Bradford-on-Avon, and a
late example at Brympton, in Somersetshire.
At Brympton there is a broad flight of steps

THE TERRACE: BRYMPTON   d'EVERCY: SOMERSET:

FIG. 42.

in the centre, and two smaller flights arranged
at right angles to the terrace near the ends.
The piers have urns, with one exception, where
there is a sun-dial on the sides of a square die.
This terrace was built at the beginning of this
century; its general effect is very good, though
the detail is poor, and the balusters are crowded
and too short. There is an excellent piece of

balustrading on either side of the entrance to
the fore court at Brympton. The balusters are
2 feet 6 high, 12 inches centre to centre, and
stand on a plinth 3 feet 3 high. It appears to
have been built towards the end of the seventeenth century. About 2 feet 9 inches to 3 feet
from the ground to the top of coping is a good
height for the balustrade ; no rule, however, can
be given for its proportions, as these depend
entirely on individual circumstances and the
scale of the work. The solid piers ought not to
be too far apart, and the relation of the solids
to the voids — that is, of the piers to the open
spaces between the balusters—is a point of the
first importance. Many variations on this
simple type of balustrade are to be found. The
terrace at Risley has obelisks on the piers and
flat stone balusters between, a feature commoner
in wood than stone. The terrace at Haddon
has six small stone arches to each bay. The
height is 3 feet, width from centre to centre
of piers 11 feet 6 inches ; the steps measure 12
inches by 5. At Kingston House, Bradford-
on-Avon, the balustrade to the terrace (much
restored) is formed of panels of stone 3½ inches
thick, pierced with open work of alternate
lozenges and ovals, with engaged balusters to
the piers, and stone urns of various designs.
At Montacute the terrace-walls on either side
of the garden at the back of the house have
simple balustrades with obelisks to the piers,

and in the centre of each side there is a curious
temple of stone ; six pillars support a circular
stone roof with a projecting cornice on brackets,
and an open cupola above, formed of three
stone ribs joining at the top and terminating in
an open ball formed of two intersecting circles
of stone. Instances of terraces with retaining
walls but no balustrade are not common.
There is an instance at Cothele, in Cornwall,
where the two upper terraces have low retaining walls of stone but no balustrade, and the
third terrace has a grass bank. The grass
bank is the better treatment and looks well
with simple flights of stone steps. The terrace
of Etwall Hall, Derbyshire, is a good example
of this.

In the French gardens the flights of steps
leading from the terrace to the lower levels
were very elaborate. In James's translation
several diagrams are given of the great French
instances. In England the steps were usually
laid out in plain rectangular flights, though
circular and curved steps were often used for
short flights. There is a good instance of
a semicircular flight at the end of the house
terrace to Eyam Hall ; and occasionally the
flight of steps widened out as it descended with
a winding balustrade, as in the steps to the
entrance of Wootton Lodge, in Staffordshire.
In the eighteenth century, when people were
more ambitious and the mason exulted in his

PITMIDDEN : ABERDEENSHIRE.

Fig. 43.

skill, flights of steps were formed of great technical difficulty. There is a remarkable instance at Prior Park. A flight of seventeen steps leads from the terrace to a landing, and then two flights of eighteen steps lead off from either side of the landing, curving round and widening out as they go. It is a masterpiece of masonry, but not very beautiful, for the staircase has an uncomfortable suggestion about it of rolling down-hill. The simpler designs are the best ; these *tours de force* of technical skill are a sure sign of failing taste.

THE OLD GARDEN & ORANGERY : MOUNT-EDGCUMBE : CORNWALL

CHAPTER IX

GARDEN ARCHITECTURE—*continued*

GARDEN-HOUSES, PERGOLAS, AVIARIES, COL-
UMBARIES, DOVE-COTES, HOT-HOUSES,
CARPENTER'S WORK, FOUNTAINS, SUN-
DIALS, STATUARY.

BANQUETING-HOUSES, gazebos, and garden-
houses, all mean pretty much the same thing in
an English garden. The origin of the word
gazebo is obscure. It was used in the last
century for the garden-house built at the corner
of the terrace at the farther end of the garden,
with outlooks to the ground or road outside.
It was in two storeys, and the first floor was
reached from the terrace. Pergola is, of course,
Italian, and signified originally a trellis of wood

at the sides and overhead, supported at the
angles by stone piers and pillars; over this
trellis was trained the vine, to form a green

FIG. 44.

arbour. "Pergola" itself
means a certain sort of grape.
The term came to be used
loosely for all covered look-
outs. Evelyn mentions a plane
and a lime-tree at Strasburg
"in which is erected a pergola
of 50 feet wide, and 8 feet
from the ground, having ten arches of 12 feet
high, all shaded with their foliage." Johnson
gives a passage where pergola is used for a part
of the banqueting-house: "He was ordained
his standing in the pergola of the banqueting-
house"—that is, in the covered approach leading up to the banqueting-house.

Few examples of older pergolas remain. They were ruth-
lessly swept away by the landscape gardeners, and it is probable that their life in its
original form would not be very
long, as the trees inevitably grew
out of shape. There is a beautiful modern pergola formed of
apple-trees at Tyninghame.

FIG. 45

The banqueting-house was a term in
common use in the seventeenth century. This
was a solid building of brick or stone, in one or

two storeys, with windows and fire-place, and
fitted up as an occasional sleeping-place as well
as for use by day.   The commonest forms were
octagon or square, with a roof constructed either
as a cupola or with two or four
gables. Its position varied. It
was usually placed at the ends of
the raised terrace at the farther
end of the garden. The example
at Place House, Tenterden, has
been already described (chap. v.) ;

Fig. 46.

other instances are shown in many of Logan's
views of the colleges of Oxford and Cambridge.
If there was a raised mount, the banqueting-
house frequently crowned its top. Markham
placed his " curious and artificial banqueting-
house " over the ascent from the lower to the

Fig. 47.

upper garden. At Penshurst
the garden-house stands to one
end of the house terrace, at
some distance in front of the
house. Worlidge says it should
be placed at an angle of the
garden, with windows and doors
commanding " every coast, the
windows to be glazed with the
clearest glass, and to have
screens of printed and painted sarcenet for day
use, and shutters of thin wainscot for night use."
It is evident that the master of the house might
occasionally lodge there for a day or two if he

wanted quiet. At the opposite end of the
terrace there was to be a similar building for
roots and seeds, which Worlidge says was
usually termed a green-house. At Montacute
the pleasure-houses are in two storeys, square,

THE BANQUET-HOUSE : SWARKESTON

Fig. 48.

with semicircular bays on all four sides, and a
slated cupola terminating in an open ball. At
Swarkestone there is a large seventeenth-century
building known as "the Balcony" which was
the banqueting-house to the Hall, now destroyed.
This building stands in the centre of the further

side of a square walled-in enclosure, measuring
76.0 paces by 61, which was once a garden.
The building consists of two square towers with
a colonnade in three bays between, open on the
ground floor ; above this was the banqueting-
room, 16.3 × 14.0, covered in by a lead flat

FIG. 49.

with a stone parapet on both sides. The left-
hand tower was occupied by the staircase, which
communicated with the first floor and the flat ;
in the right-hand tower were rooms in three
storeys. The towers are covered with lead
cupolas. It is quite possible that the triangular
lodge at Rushton, built by Sir Thomas Tresham,
was intended to be used as a banqueting-house,

and there is little doubt that this was the intention of the building planned on pentagons at Amesbury, in Wilts. Over the door is the inscription, " Diana, her house," and the date. Of eighteenth-century work there are still a good many instances left. At Boxted Hall, in

GARDEN-HOUSE ON THE WEY, SURREY:

FIG. 50.

Suffolk, the garden-house stands at one end of the fruit garden. The ground floor is open in front, with entrance in the centre between two stone columns, which support the upper storey, and wood balustrades between the columns and the wall. The upper storey is of brick with stone quoins, and has a gable roof, tiled, with a semi-circular window.

There is a good instance of a brick gazebo on the Wey canal, about 6 miles from Weybridge, dating probably from the beginning of the eighteenth century. This is a large square building with heavy projecting eaves, and a curiously hipped tile roof. It stands at one end of a raised walk some 7 feet high, with a solid

brick retaining wall and parapet, which overlooks
the garden on one side and the canal on the other.
A narrow strip of grass planted with flowers

ISAAC WALTON'S FISHING-HOUSE : DOVEDALE

FIG. 51.

separates the wall from the canal.   In Lea Park
Lane, Guildford, there is a two-storey garden-
house, since converted to other uses, with a roof
of similar design.   Buildings such as Walton

and Cotton's fishing-house at Beresford, in
Derbyshire (1674) (in stone and slate), and the
water pavilion at Wrest (brick with lead dome)
are to all intents and purposes garden-houses.
After the middle of the eighteenth century the
unpretentious comfort of these sober buildings
did not satisfy the taste of the time. Greek
temples and hermitages were thought more
elegant, and these in turn gave way to the rustic
summer-house with its draughts, its earwigs, and
its beetles.

In the sixteenth century aviaries were occasionally built in the greater gardens. No
instances of these are left ; but a curious
account of the aviary at Kenilworth is preserved in the description of the Queen's enter-
tainment at Kenilworth in 1575. This aviary
was 20 feet high, 30 long, and 14 broad.
At about 5 feet from the ground there were
four windows in the front and two at each end,
with mullions, transoms, architraves, and circular
heads. Between the windows there were piers
with flat pilasters carrying an elaborate cornice,
the frieze of which was decorated with imitations
of precious stones, diamonds, rubies, emeralds,
and sapphires, carved and painted. The building was not roofed in, and the windows had no
glass, but instead fine wire netting was strained
across the top and behind the windows. In
the walls at the back niches were formed for
the birds to roost in. The inside was planted

DOVECOTE AT ROUSHAM:OXFORD

Fig. 52.

with holly-trees. Columbaries or pigeon-houses
were, of course, quite indispensable to every
country house. These were always placed at
some distance from the house, and seldom inside
the garden-walls. They were usually square or
octagon, with gable roofs and a weather-cock
or cupola forming a small open-air dove-cote at
the top. Circular pigeon-houses are less common. There is an instance at Rousham in
the rose garden. The interior was arranged
with tiers of nesting-places built in the walls,
and in some cases, as at Melton Hall, in Norfolk,
and at Athelhampton, in Dorset, a revolving post
stood in a socket in the centre with a projecting arm, to which a ladder was hung. By
turning round the post access could be got to
any part of the building. Evelyn mentions
a " pigeon-house of most laudable example "
at Godstone, in Surrey. Many of these pigeon-
houses — such as the great square one at
Southstoke, near Goring—are so exceedingly
picturesque that there seems no reason for
excluding them from the garden, and they
are referred to for this reason, though, strictly
speaking, they are outside the range of garden
architecture. The ordinary barrel dove-cote
on its high post was often put up in the
garden. In an old garden near Southwater
a dove-cote such as this forms the centre-piece
of a square walled garden, with straight grass
paths leading up to a circle in the centre,

and the effect is very good. In Badeslade's
view of Sundridge Place, in Kent (1720), the
dove-cote is shown standing in the centre of the
fish-pond. The water-floor was
occupied by the ducks ; above this
was a room with a balcony all
round, and steps up from the
water ; and the upper part was
pierced with holes and perches for the
pigeons. A large octagonal wooden
dove-cote on a wood trestle is shown
in Logan's view of St. John's, Oxford.

Fig. 53.

Hot-houses and orangeries do not seem to
have been in use in England till the end of
the seventeenth century. One of the earliest
hot-houses is described by Olivier de Serres.
It was built for the Elector Palatine of Heidelberg, and appears to have been a movable
structure formed with great wooden shutters
and windows. Evelyn mentions the orangery
at Ham House ; but this may have been only
a plantation, and perhaps does not refer to the
existing orange-house. Neither Worlidge nor
London and Wise refer to the subject at all.
The first orange-house with a glass roof is said
to have been built at Wollaton in 1696.
Evelyn, however, writing in 1677, mentions
the conservatory at Euston, "some hundred
feete long, adorn'd with mapps, as the other
side is with heads of Cæsars, all cut in alabaster."
In the eighteenth century a good many orange-

houses were built, in most cases from the designs of architects, and therefore with some regard to their effect. Sir W. Chambers's building at Kew, now used as a museum of woods, or the orangery at Mount Edgcumbe show that a conservatory or hot-house need not be the hideous thing to which the gardener has brought it. The hot-house or conservatory is necessary no doubt, but it is surely not necessary to reduce the mullions to mere strips of wood, and the power of the sun would not be seriously reduced by a few sash-bars instead of those vast sheets of blazing glass which inevitably spoil the beauty of any garden.

The carpenter found plenty of work to do in the old formal garden. In the first place he had to make the solid frames of wood, the *deambulationes ligneae horti*, which were necessary for the green walks and arbours. These frames were made of timber, wrought and square, nailed or pinned together, and painted green, with curved ribs for the arched tops. Instances are shown in De Caux's views of Wilton and several of Logan's plates, such as the view of Wadham Gardens. These framings became very elaborate at the end of the seventeenth century. Porticoes, colonnades with cornices and pediments, niches and shells, domes, lanterns, and other architectural details were carried out in wainscot and deal, and the plain spaces filled in with trellis-work of

wainscot oak, 1 inch square, framed into
chequers, 6 or 7 inches square, and covered
with roses, jessamine, and honeysuckle, or with
lime, elm, or hornbeam. Evelyn describes a
cupola in Sir Henry Capell's garden at Kew,
"made with pole work, between two elmes,
at the end of a walk, which, being covered by
plashing the elmes to them, is very pretty."
James gives a plate of designs for this work
which are not attractive. It was costly and
very soon fell out of repair, and was abandoned
without much loss to the garden. Plain
wooden arbours of planks or stout oak framing are often shown in old views of the
seventeenth century, but no instances remain
except one at Canons Ashby, which might
date from the end of the seventeenth century.
These were different in intention from the
garden-house, as they were only made to
shelter the garden-seat. There are two
eighteenth - century instances at Melbourne.

Worlidge says that the seats should
be of wood, painted white or
green, and set in niches in the
garden-wall, or at the end of
garden walks. They might be
circular or square in plan. In
the first case, half the circle

FIG. 54.

would be inside the niche, the other half
outside it, covered in by a cupola with a
cornice on three or four columns of wood or

stone, the roof to be covered with lead,
slates, or shingles. If they were square, about
2 feet would go inside the niche of the wall,
and as much outside. The details of the seats
would be much the same as that of the ordinary
seventeenth-century settle. There is a good
example at the end of the raised grass walk at
Bingham Melcombe, in Dorset. Garden-seats
of good simple design continued to be made till
the beginning of the last century. The backs,
instead of being framed in solid, were formed
with a trellis of bars about an inch square,
framed into panels of various design. The
fashion appears to have been started by Sir
William Chambers, who took it from the
Chinese, though something of the same sort
had been done before in wooden balustrades to
stairs. Of wooden fences several varieties were
in use. The commonest were palings—that is,
pieces of wood about 3 to 4 inches wide and
3 to 4 feet high, with variously shaped heads,
nailed to two rails. Worlidge gives as a variation a palisade of boards turned edgewise to the
garden, the rails passing through the boards.
The heads were to be shaped into two square
spikes, with a space between. These ought to
be raised above the ground on a low brick
plinth. Wooden balustrades were rarely used.
They are shown in Logan's view of Trinity,
Cambridge. A common form of fencing,
shown in Logan's views of Oxford and

Cambridge, consisted of a stout single rail, framed into square posts, the upper part of which was turned as a baluster or finial. At Tissington there is a good wooden railing next the park, formed of a stout moulded rail at top and bottom mortised into solid posts 1 foot by $4\frac{1}{2}$ inches. These posts are shaped like balusters. The wooden gates were often solid and panelled, and differ little from the doors of the time. The upper panel was often filled with vertical bars. There is a good example of a seventeenth-century wooden gate at Eyam Hall, and another at Canons Ashby. For large gates, iron was more often used.

The orange-trees which were set out on the terrace stood in cases, in order to be moved into shelter in winter. London and Wise recommended that the bottom should be perforated and filled in with oyster shells and potsherds, to let the water get away, and each side should be made with hinges to open, in order to get at the "hard, crusty, reticulated roots," and to water them and put in fresh earth. They give 18 × 18 inches to each side as a dimension, but this is much too small. In the gardens at the back of the Hôtel de Ville, at Rouen, there are some good examples which measure 5 feet by 5, with angle posts 4 inches square, and planking $1\frac{1}{2}$ inches thick. All the sides are hinged.

Fountains of every description were always

THE GREEN COURT : CANONS ASHBY : NORTHAMPTONSHIRE

Fig. 55.

used in the garden. The beautiful conduit
shown in the garden scene from "The Romance
of the Rose," with its marble basin and runnel of
water in a marble channel, shows its use in the
mediæval garden. The Rev. Samuel Pegge,
who wrote an account of Bolsover Castle in
1785, mentions that at Leigh Priory there used
to be a fountain in brick "of several stories,"
and probably dating from the time of Henry
VIII. At Nonsuch there was a marble fountain with a pelican carved above it, and fountains were made at Theobalds and Greenwich
for James I. The fountain at Kenilworth had
an octagonal basin 4 feet high, and large enough
for carp, in the centre of which were two
athletes of white marble, standing back to back,
and carrying a ball "3 feet over," with the
bear and ragged staff at the top. The sides of
the basin were carved with Neptune, "Thetis in
her chariot, drawn by her dolphins, there Triton
by his fishes, here Proteus herding his sea-bulls,
then Doris and her daughters, solacing on sea
and sands," and with "whales and whirlpools,
sturgeons, Tunnys, conchs and wealks." In
the seventeenth century the ingenuity of the
designer was spent in practical jokes—such as
fountains which drenched you with water if you
stepped on a hidden spring. The copper-tree
at Chatsworth is a bad instance. But besides
these, water-toys were much in fashion. Both
Solomon and Isaac de Caux invented various

curious devices for waterwork. Solomon published his book in French at Frankfort in
1615. It contained designs for water organs
and imitations of the notes of birds, and designs
for raising water by means of air-tight vessels
placed in the sun, made of copper, with burning
glasses fixed in the sides. The work of Isaac
de Caux was translated by John Leak (London,
1659). Plate XIV. gives a method for "divers
birds, which shall sing diversely when an owl
turns towards them, and when the said owl
turns back again they shall cease their playing."
Plate XV. gives an engine by which "Galatea
shall be presented, which shall be drawn upon
the water by two Dolphins, going in a right
line and returning of herself, while a Cyclops
plaies upon a Flagolett." Evelyn in 1662 says
that at Hampton Court, "in ye garden is a
rich and noble fountain, with syrens, statues,
etc., cast in copper by Fanelli, but no plenty of
water." Boecklern's *Hydragogica Nova*, published at Nuremberg in 1664, contains many
designs for fountains, some of them in copper
and lead. Several varieties of fountains with
illustrations are given in Worlidge's book,
including one or two unseemly practical jokes.
Switzer wrote an *Introduction to a general
System of Hydrostatics and Hydraulics . . .
for the Watering of Noblemen's and Gentlemen's
Seats, Buildings, Gardens*, etc., but Switzer is
exceedingly dull, and his designs are detestable.

FOUNTAIN AT BOLSOVER: DERBYSHIRE

Fig. 56.

In many of Kip's views fountains of statuary are shown. One of the largest was at Longleat. Another famous fountain, that at Bolsover, is still left, though in a mutilated state. It was described by Pegge as consisting of an octagon reservoir, 6 feet deep, in which stood the fountain with engaged semicircular pedestals carrying griffins. In the angle were satyrs, sitting astride of eagles; in the sides (of the reservoir) were arched niches with busts of eight of the Roman emperors, made of alabaster. The centre-piece consisted of a square rusticated pedestal carrying a circular basin; above this was a figure of Venus in alabaster, standing on a pedestal with one foot raised. This fountain was fed from a lead cistern 20 feet square. The objection to fountains on such an elaborate scale as this is that they are very expensive to maintain, and without a constant supply of water they soon become squalid. The neglected fountains in the groves at Versailles are most melancholy to look upon. The fine marble curbs are falling to pieces, and, where bright water should be playing, weeds and grass are forcing their way through the cracks of the broken pavement. It is wiser to keep the fountain simple, and to be content with a plain well-built basin of brick or stone and some little figure in lead, as at Melbourne.

Sun-dials have always held an honoured place

SUNDIAL : WREST : BEDFORDSHIRE

Fig. 57.

in the formal garden, sometimes on the terrace, sometimes as the centre of some little garden of lilies and sweet flowers. Every one loves them because they suggest the human interest of the garden, the long continuity of tradition which has gone before, and will outlive us. "Pereunt et imputantur," "Scis horas, nescis horam," "Sine sole sileo," "Horas non numero nisi serenas," "I mark time, dost thou?" Such were some of the mottoes used to point the lesson of the sun-dial. Instances of eighteenth-century sun-dials are still fairly common. There is a graceful example on the side terrace at Hampton Court and another rather similar instance at Wrest. At Wroxton Abbey, in Oxfordshire, there is a remarkable sun-dial; the plate is fixed on a moulded circular top, carried by four draped female figures, who stand on a square pedestal, the angles of which are decorated with rams' heads and swags of fruit and flowers. The pedestal stands on a circular step. The whole is executed in white marble, and, unless it is an importation, appears to date from the end of the eighteenth century, though the base looks much earlier. The dial plates were always of bronze, many of them very well engraved, and were, of course, designed by specialists who understood the intricate process of dialing, whether for side or top plates. In Scotland and the north of England sun-dials were often made of stone polygonal balls set on a pedestal

SUNDIAL AT CHEESEBURN
& NORTHUMBERLAND

Fig. 58.

and carved into various mysterious scoops and hollows, which look exceedingly picturesque, but to the lay mind are unintelligible. There is a curious instance in the market-place at Wilton, apparently dating from the seventeenth century.

Statuary has never played such an important part in the English garden as it did on the continent, and this is probably due not merely to difference of climate, but to the greater sobriety of English taste. Wood, stone, marble, bronze, and lead have all been used for the purpose in England. The wooden beasts in Henry VIII.'s garden at Hampton Court have been already mentioned; these were painted no doubt in all sorts of cheerful colours, anyhow in red and green and white. Wood, however, is not a very suitable material for garden sculpture. Unless its forms are very simple, the sun and rain soon destroy its effect. Marble was often used in the more important seventeenth-century gardens, not only for fountains but for pieces of isolated statuary. In the gardens at Kenilworth in the centre of each of the four plots there stood obelisks 15 feet high, formed of a single piece of porphyry. The obelisks stood on a base 2 feet square, and were pierced, and carried a ball at the top 10 inches in diameter. At Wilton there were statues of Bacchus and Flora in white marble 8 feet high. Fortunately marble was found too

WHITE MARBLE SUNDIAL
WROXTON ABBEY : OXFORDSHIRE

Fig. 59.

costly for outside work. Marble statuary is a mistake in an English garden. To attain its full effect it wants strong sunlight, a clear dry light, and a cloudless sky. In the soft light

and nebulous atmosphere of the north marble looks forlorn and out of place. It does not colour like stone, and the qualities of which it is most capable—such as refinements of contour and modelling — are simply lost under an English sky. The same objection applies to bronze casts. Apart from their cost, bronze figures always retain their original hardness of form. They do not lend themselves to the

LEAD FIGURE OF PERSEUS
MELBOURNE: DERBYSHIRE

Fig. 60.

modelling of nature ; they do not grow in with nature, as stone or lead. To the sculptor this would be a strong point in its favour, as, of course, it should be where houses and palaces and cities are concerned. But in the garden one wants something different ; man's handiwork should be in suggestion rather than in evidence, and bronze figures are too trenchant, too strong, if you like, to take their place among the gentler beauties of the garden. The only point in their favour is the beautiful patina they may acquire with age. Bronze or brass figures, as the older writers call them, were, however, occasionally used. At Wilton there was a statue of the gladiator in "brass," and James in his translation mentions such statues as common.

Stone is the proper material for carved work in an English garden, especially Portland stone. It is hard and weathers well, and few if any stones profit so much by exposure to the sun and rain. The harshness of its outlines becomes softened by time, and it will take on the most delicate colours, from the green stains of the pedestal to the pure white of the statue that gleams from under the deep canopy of yew. Instances of stone statuary in gardens earlier than the eighteenth century are not common in England. When the old formal gardens were destroyed by landscape gardeners, the stone terminal figures, the statues of Pan and Diana, were broken up to make the paths, or pitched aside into builders' yards, where a few melancholy survivors may still be found. Switzer, writing in 1718, refers to the great skill of the masons of his time, and even suggested that it would be a "work worthy of the Royal munificence to erect an Acamedy (*sic*), as is common in all other countries, especially in France and Italy, for the improvement of statuary. At present,"

STONE VASE AT HAMPTON COURT

Fig. 61.

he continues, " we have only a few leaden tame copies."

Of all the materials, that most commonly used was lead. It was abundant in England and easily cast, and throughout the eighteenth century, particularly in the early part of it, leadwork was a very flourishing and important industry. It was used in the garden for tanks, cisterns, figures, and fountains, and vases of every description. There is a remarkable instance of a lead tank at St. Fagan's, near Cardiff, in front of the house. It is octagonal, about 8 feet in diameter and about 4 feet high ; the sides are decorated with a band of foliage and arcading, such as is commonly found in seventeenth-century panelling. Lead was used for statues of every degree of importance. The equestrian figure of George I. at Canons, known as the Golden Horse, was of lead gilt all over. Statues from the antique were reproduced in lead—such as the figures in the courtyard at Knole, or the flying Mercury at Melbourne. Diana and her stag, the Seasons, Flora or Pan, the garden god, were favourite subjects for lead figures. Original work was also done, such as figures of haymakers, skaters, and gamekeepers. At Canons Ashby, at the end of the avenue leading up to the fore court, there is a lead figure of a shepherd in the dress of the eighteenth century playing on a flute ; the figure is about 5 feet high. On a terrace over-

hanging the Ouse at Nun Monkton, in Yorkshire, there are set out allegorical figures of lead
with gilded trappings. There are six lead
figures over life size at Hardwick Hall. Four

LEAD FIGURE OF CUPID
MELBOURNE : DERBY.

FIG. 62.

of these stand on
pedestals in niches of
the yew-hedge round
the great circle at the
intersection of the
paths ; one represents
painting, another a
young man playing a
shepherd's pipe, the
third a female figure
with a violin, the fourth
a figure with a trum-
pet. The gardens at
Melbourne are rich in
lead figures ; there are
two of blacks carrying
vases on salvers, rather
like the one in the
Temple gardens.

These are painted black with white drapery.
Besides these there are heroic figures of Perseus
and Andromeda beside the great water, and
several cupids in pairs and single. The single
figures are about 2 feet high. One has fallen
off his tree, another is flying upward, another
shooting, another shaping his bow with a
spokeshave. All of these are painted and

LEAD VASE AT HAMPTON COURT.

Fig. 63.

some covered with stone-dust to imitate stone, a gratuitous insult to lead, which will turn to a delicate silvery gray, if left to its own devices ; but there is no doubt that these figures were often gilt and painted different colours. Melbourne also possesses the most magnificent lead vase in England. It stands on a stone pedestal some 5 feet 3 from the ground. The vase itself, which is over 7 feet high, is supported by four monkeys and richly ornamented ; its modelling is admirable.

Other good instances are to be found at Hampton Court, Wrest, and Penshurst. At Sprotborough, in Yorkshire, there are some vases, apparently from the same mould as those at Penshurst. At the same place there are two lead toads about 9 inches long, said to have belonged to the fountains, and no doubt suggested by those at Versailles. At Wootton, in a fountain behind the house, there is a lead duck suspended so as to swim on the water and spout water from its bill. There are many other instances of the use of lead for the details of garden ornament. It is a material that might well be brought into use again for the same purpose. It is durable and inexpensive, though it must not be used in a niggardly way. Lead statues very easily lose their centre of gravity, and when once they begin to move over they become exceedingly comic. The flying Mercury at

LEAD VASE : PENSHURST, KENT

Fig. 64.

Melbourne is slowly taking a header into the grass in front of his pedestal. Lead . has a beautiful colour of its own, and it is not, like bronze or marble, a material too grand and sumptuous for use in the quiet English garden. These figures are invaluable for giving a point of interest here and there. They are charming in summer, when "the lilac waves its plumes above them, and the syringa thrusts its flowers under their arms," [1] and when autumn has dropped its last red leaf at their feet, they will carry the memory of summer through the dreary days of winter.

[1] W. R. Lethaby. Mr. Lethaby says that during the War of Independence many of those lead figures were exported to America as "works of art" in order to be melted down into bullets.

CHAPTER X

CONCLUSION

THE disregard of conditions which the land-scape gardener shows in dealing with the house and garden is even more conspicuous in his treatment of public grounds. For some inscrutable reason the laying out of public grounds is usually left either to the engineer or to the landscape gardener. The engineer is, no doubt, a man of ability and attainment, but there is nothing in his training to qualify him to deal with a problem which is in the main artistic; and the landscape gardener makes it his business to dispense with serious design. The result is that our public spaces are seldom laid out on any principle at all. For instance, a London square is an entirely artificial affair. It is bounded by rectangular blocks of buildings, and straight roads and fences. It would only be reasonable to adhere to this simple motive; but hand this over to the landscape gardener and he will at once set to work to contradict the whole character of the place by means of irregular curves and irrelevant hummocks. His dislike of a simple straight line and a plain piece of grass amounts almost to a mania. In Bloomsbury, till within the last few years, there existed a good old-fashioned square garden, laid out in four grass plots, with a lime walk and a border of flowers running round the sides. It was restful and pleasant to look at. The grass plots were good for lawn-tennis and the lime walks kindly to the citizen ; but the landscape gardener appeared on the scene and speedily put all this to rights. He cut up the grass plots and destroyed two sides of the lime walk, and heaped up some mounds, and made the most curiously un-reasonable paths ; and went his way, having destroyed one of the few square gardens in London with any pretence to design. Instead of trying to treat the square as a whole, or, better still, instead of leaving it alone, he de-liberately turned his back on the adjacent archi-tecture, and produced a result which has no dis-tinction but that of immense vulgarity.

Much more might be done in the way of planting avenues of trees along the approaches to towns and in the towns themselves. Evelyn mentions the road from Heidelberg to Darm-stadt, which was planted all the way with walnuts, and an avenue of 4 leagues long and 50 paces wide, " planted with young oaklings, as straight

as a line, from the city of Utrecht to Amers-
foort." The road from Hoorn to Alkmaar, in
North Holland, and from Hoorn to Enkhuizen,
passes for miles under an avenue of elms. "Is
there," Evelyn says, "a more ravishing or
delightful object, than to behold some entire
streets and whole towns planted with these
lime-trees in even lines before their doors, so
as they seem like cities in a wood?" Mr.
Robinson's views to the contrary are significant. In his *Garden Design*, p. 50, he asserts
that "the ugliest things in the fair land
of France are the ugly old lines of clipt
limes which deface many French towns." In
regard to this assertion, I would only repeat,[1]
that the depth of colour, the play of re-
flected light, the extreme brilliancy of the
isolated spots of sunshine, which result from
these close-clipt masses of leafage, must surely
appeal to a person of quite ordinary sensibility. But the point of serious moment in
Mr. Robinson's pronouncement is its hopeless
modernism in the worst sense. It shows an
insensibility to what has been done in the past,
and an unconsciousness of a whole world of
thought, which together constitute one of the
most fatal tendencies of modern design. Out
of a mind well stored with knowledge and tradi-

---

[1] Preface to the second edition of this book. I may also refer to
a paper on "Public Spaces, Parks, and Gardens," in a series of lectures
on the building and decoration of cities, by members of the Arts and
Crafts Society (Rivington, 1897).

tion good original ideas may come, but what are we to expect from a mind stored with the ideas of the Great Exhibition of 1851? We are to expect exactly what we have got in most of our modern parks and public gardens, and we cannot feel very sanguine as to any prospects of improvement. The London County Council have shown a wise anxiety to secure public spaces whenever possible, but when they have got them their advisers seem very uncertain as to how they should deal with them. They waste the public money in humps and earthworks, and economise in kiosques and cast-iron fountains, and this, though there are admirable models to follow in the gardens of the Luxembourg and the Tuileries and in most of the important cities of Europe. Nowhere is the provincialism of modern English thought more clearly shown than in our State and municipal dealings with art.

In dealing with great spaces the landscape gardener seems to have little idea of mass. He is for ever breaking up the outline with little knots of trees, and reducing the size of his grounds by peppering them all over with shrubs. The consequence is that though one may feel weary with traversing his interminable paths, no permanent impression of size is left on the mind. Such a place, for instance, as Battersea Park is like a bad piece of architecture full of details which stultify each other. The

only good point in it is the one avenue,
and this leads to nowhere. If this park had
been planted out with groves and avenues
of limes, like the boulevard at Avallon, or the
squares at Vernon, or even like the east side
of Hyde Park between the Achilles statue
and the Marble Arch, at least one definite
effect would have been reached. There might
have been shady walks, and noble walls of
trees, instead of the spasmodic futility of
Battersea Park, and without pedantry the
principles of formal garden design should
be applied to public grounds and parks.
A dominant idea should control the general
scheme. Merely to introduce so many
statues or plaster casts is to begin at the
wrong end. These are the accidents of the
system, not the system itself, and this is why
the attempt at formal gardening at the head
of the Serpentine was such a failure. The
details were not particularly well designed,
but even if they had been, it was essentially
inartistic to plump them down in the midst of
incongruous surroundings.

Perhaps of all the unsatisfactory public places
in England the worst is the public cemetery.
Here again one finds the same disregard of
decent order, the same hatred of simplicity, the
same meanness of imagination. Here, if anywhere, all pettiness, all banalities should be
avoided. We want rest, even if it is sombre in

its severity ; but instead we are offered narrow winding roads and broken pillars under weeping willows, everything that can suggest the ghastly paraphernalia of the undertaker. Why not have long walks of yew at once, with cypress-trees or junipers ? But the landscape gardener is nothing if not " natural," and so he gives us a bad copy of an ill-chosen subject. Only nature left alone can create her own particular beauty, and only in the churchyard of some far-away village can her work be judged, where the grass grows tenderly over the dead, and the graves are shaded by immemorial yews, and the sun-dial patiently wears away on its gray stone base while it counts the silent hours.

As was pointed out in an earlier chapter, the landscape gardener attempts to establish a sort of hierarchy of nature, based on much the same principle as that which distinguishes a gentleman by his incapacity to do any useful work. Directly it is proved that a plant or a tree is good for food, it is expelled from the flower garden without any regard to its intrinsic beauty. The hazel-hedge has gone, and the apple-tree has long been banished from the flowers. Of all the trees an apple-tree in full bloom, or ripe in autumn, is perhaps the loveliest. Trained as an espalier it makes a beautiful hedge, and set out as in an orchard it lets the sun play through its leaves and

chequer with gold the green velvet of the grass
in a way that no other tree will quite allow.
Nothing can be more beautiful than some of
the walks under the apple-trees in the gardens
at Penshurst. Yet the landscape gardener
would shudder at the idea of planting a grove
or hedge of apple-trees in his garden. Instead
of this he will give you a conifer or a monkey-
puzzler, though the guelder-rose grows wild in
the meadow and the spindle-tree in the wood,
and the rowan, the elder, and the white-thorn ;
and the wild cherry in autumn fires the wood-
land with its crimson and gold. Every one
admires these as a matter of proper sensibility
to nature, but it does not seem to occur to
people that they would grow with as little
difficulty in a garden, and at the very smallest
expense. It would undoubtedly injure the
business of the nursery gardener to allow that
they were possible. Again, the pear-tree and
the chequer-tree, the quince, the medlar, and the
mulberry are surely entitled by their beauty
to a place in the garden. It is only since
nature has been taken in hand by the landscapist and taught her proper position that
these have been excluded. When there was
no talk about nature, and man had not learnt
to consider himself as something detached from
nature and altogether superior, the fruit-
tree was counted among the beauties of the
garden. It is of fruit-trees that Homer

tells us in the garden of Alcinous : "Without
the palace, near the doors, was a great garden,
four acres by four, and round it on every side
was driven a fence. There grew tall trees and
beautiful pears and pomegranates, and apple-
trees with gleaming fruit, and luscious figs and
teeming olive-trees." [1] Or again, in the ground
of a mediæval tapestry all beautiful flowers and
fruits grow together, the strawberry next the
violet, and columbines among the raspberries,
and fair roses twine among the apple boughs.
So again with flowers : "The dahlia has
banished the hollyhock, with its old friend the
sunflower, into the cottage garden, where it
still flanks the little walk that leads from the
wicket to the porch—not the only instance in
which our national taste has been redeemed by
the cottage against the vulgar pretensions of
luxury and wealth." [2] It is more of this un-
sophisticated liking for everything that is
beautiful that ought to be allowed full play
in the gardens ; less of the pedantry that lays
down rules about nature and is at heart in-
different to the beauty about which it preaches.

If there were any truth in his cant about
nature would the landscape gardener bed out

[1] *Odyssey*, vii. 112-116—

ἔκτοσθεν δ' αὐλῆς μέγας ὄρχατος ἄγχι θυράων
τετράγυος· περὶ δ' ἕρκος ἐλήλαται ἀμφοτέρωθεν.
ἔνθα δὲ δένδρεα μακρὰ πεφύκει τηλεθόωντα
ὄγχναι καὶ ῥοιαί, καὶ μηλέαι ἀγλαόκαρποι
συκαῖ τε γλυκεραί, καὶ ἐλαῖαι τηλεθόωσαι.

[2] James, in *The Carthusian*.

asters and geraniums, would he make the lawn hideous with patches of brilliant red varied by streaks of purple blue, and add his finishing touch in the magenta of his choicest dahlia? Would he plant them in patterns of stars and lozenges and tadpoles? would he border them with paths of asphalt? Would he not rather fill his borders with every kind of beautiful flower that he might delight in? It is impossible to take his professions seriously when he so flies in the face of nature, when he transplants exotics into impossible conditions, when rarity, difficulty, and expense of production are his tests of the value of a flower. The beauty that he claims for his garden is not his but that of the flowers, the grass, the sunlight, and the cloud, which no amount of bad design can utterly destroy.

A garden is so much an individual affair—it should show so distinctly the idiosyncrasy of its owner—that it would be useless to offer any hints as to its details. The brief sketch which has been given of the development of the formal garden will indicate the very wide field of design which it includes, and the abuses and extravagance which led to its decay and ultimate extinction. The study of its history will at least show the dangers to be avoided, and they can be summarised in the faults of over-elaboration and affectation. The characteristic of the old formal garden, the garden of Mark-

ham and Lawson, was its exceeding simplicity.
The primary purpose of a garden as a place
of retirement and seclusion, a place for quiet
thought and leisurely enjoyment, was kept
steadily in view. The grass and the yew-trees

PENSHURST PLACE : KENT : A MODERN GARDEN

Fig. 65.

were trimmed close to gain their full beauty
from the sunlight. Sweet kindly flowers filled
the knots and borders. Peacocks and pigeons
brightened the terraces and lawns. The paths
were straight and ample, the garden-house
solidly built and comfortable; everything was
reasonable and unaffected. But this simple

genuine delight in nature and art became
feebler as the seventeenth century grew older.
Gardening became the fashionable art, and this
was the golden age for professional gardeners ;
but the real pleasure of it was gone. Rows of
statues were introduced from the French, costly
architecture superseded the simple terrace, intricate parterres were laid out from gardeners'
pattern books, and meanwhile the flowers were
forgotten. It was well that all this pomp
should be swept away. We do not want this
extravagant statuary, this aggressive prodigality.

But though one would admit that in its
decay the formal garden became unmanageable
and absurd, the abuse is no argument against
the use. An attempt has been made in this
book to show the essential reasonableness of
the principles of Formal Gardening, and the
sanity of its method when properly handled.
The long yew - hedge is clipped and shorn
because we want its firm boundary lines and
the plain mass of its colour ; the grass bank
is formed into a definite slope to attain the
beauty of close-shaven turf at varied angles
with the light. The broad grass walk, with
its paved footpath in the centre, is cool to walk
upon in summer and dry on the pavement in
winter ; and the flower border on either side
is planted with every kind of delightful flower,
so that the refinements of its colour may be
enjoyed all through the summer. It is not

SUNDIAL IN A SCOTCH GARDEN

Fig. 66.

filled with bedded-out plants, because for long
months it would be bare and desolate, because
there is no pleasure in a solid spot of hard
blazing colour, and because there is delight in
the associations of the sweet old-fashioned
flowers.   There is music in their very names :—

> " In the garden, what in the garden ?
> Jacob's ladder, and Solomon's seal, [1]
> And love lies bleeding, with none to heal,
> In the garden."

Gillyflowers and columbines, sweet-williams,
sweet-johns, hollyhocks and marigolds, ladies'
slipper, London pride, bergamot and dittany,
fine-haired jacint, pease everlasting, bachelor's
buttons, flower of Bristol, love in a mist, apple
of love, crown imperial, shepherd's needle, sage
of Bethlehem, floramor or flower-gentle, good-
night at noone, herb Paris, Venus's looking-
glass—these are a few old names to contrast
with the horrors of a nursery gardener's catalogue, and these, too, are the sort of flowers for
the garden.   The formal garden lends itself
readily to designs of smaller gardens within the
garden—such as gardens of roses and lilies, or
of poppies, or " coronary gardens," as they used
to be called, filled with all flowers for garlands,
such as Spenser names :—

---

[1] See Gerard's *Herbal*, chap. 324.   Gerard remarks that this flower
was a sovereign remedy for any bruises due to " women's wilfulness in
stumbling upon their hastie husbands' fists."

" Bring hither the pinke and purple columbine,
  With gillyflowers,
Bring sweet carnations, and sops in wine,[1]
  Worne of paramours,
Strew me the ground with daffa-down-dillies
And cowslips, and king-cups, and loved lilies,
  The pretty paunce
  And the chevisaunce
Shall match with the faire flower de luce." [2]

These and many another fancy, such as English men and women loved three hundred years ago, might be carried out, not for archæology, not for ostentation, but because they give real pleasure and delight. This, after all, is the only principle. It is nothing to us that the French did this or the Italians that ; the point is, what has been done in England, what has been loved here, by us and by those before us. The best English tradition has always been on the side of refinement and reserve ; it has loved beauty—not the obvious beauty of the south, but the charm and tenderness, the inexpressible sweetness of faces that fill the memory like half-remembered music. This is the feeling that one would wish to see realised in the garden again, not the coarse facility that overwhelms with its astonishing cleverness, but the delicate touch of the artist, the finer scholarship which loves the past and holds thereby the key to its meaning.

[1] " Sops in wine " is given by Gerard in his chapter on Clover Gilly-flowers as a variety of that flower.
[2] Iris.

APPENDIX I

EVELYN'S GARDEN BOOK

Bray's *Memoirs of Evelyn*, vol. ii. p. 107.—"Amongst Mr. E.'s papers was found this printed sketch of the intended work above mentioned under the title of

ELYSIUM BRITANNICUM

In Three Books

Præmissis præ mittendis, etc.

Book I

CHAP.

1. A garden derived and defined, with its distinction and sorts.
2. Of a gardener, and how he is to be qualified.
3. Of the principles and elements in generall.
4. Of the fire.
5. Of the aire and winde.
6. Of the water.
7. Of the earth.
8. Of the celestial influences, particularly the sun and moon, and of the climates.
9. Of the four seasons.
10. Of the mould and soil of a garden.
11. Of the composts and stercoration.
12. Of the generation of plants.

Book II

directing what he is to do monethly and what flowers are in prime.

Book III

APPENDIX II

COUNT TALLARD'S GARDEN AT
NOTTINGHAM

MARSHAL COUNT TALLARD, the commander of the French forces, was taken prisoner at the battle of Blenheim, or Hochstedt as the Germans called it, and interned at Nottingham. London and Wise laid out a garden for him in 1706, of which they have left a detailed description in *The Retired Gard'ner*. The reproduction is taken from the plate in *Les Délices de la Grande Bretagne*. In front of the house was a terrace about 60 feet long and 14 wide. In front of this was a parterre of grass-work, generally called a "fund of grass," laid out in cut-work (*gazon coupé*) all in grass. The paths of this parterre were filled in with different coloured materials, such as brick dust, coal slag, sand, etc. There seem to have been no flowers to this parterre, except some plants in pots, and this particular part of the design sounds rather puerile.

Above this parterre on the right was another parterre with a grass terrace on a higher level. Below it and in front of it was a third parterre in grass, reached by a flight of seven steps. At the farther end of the garden was a raised walk of grass, with a border of flowers on one side, and pyramidal trees and flower-pots on the other. At the left-hand corner was a banqueting-house, reached from the raised walk, with a room under it, entered from the level of the third parterre. The walks were about 8 feet wide ; the entire garden appears only to have measured 150 feet

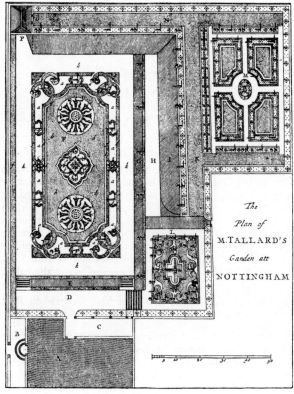

The
Plan of
M. TALLARD'S
Garden att
NOTTINGHAM

FIG. 67.

long by 140 wide in the widest part. It is interesting as a contemporary account of a small town garden written by the actual designers.

APPENDIX III

LIST OF PRINCIPAL WORKS REFERRED TO

"THE Romance of the Rose." Harleian MS. 4425.

DR. ANDREW BORDE—"The Boke for to lerne a man to be wyse in buyldyng of his house." 1540. 8vo.

THOMAS HILL—"A most briefe and pleasaunt treatyse teachynge how to dress, sowe, and set a garden." London, 1563. 8vo.

—— "The proffitable Arte of Gardening." London, 1568. 8vo.

DIDYMUS MOUNTAINE — "The Gardener's Labyrinth." London, 1577. 4to.

OLIVIER DE SERRES—"Le Théâtre d'Agriculture et mesnage des Champs." Paris, 1603. Folio.

BACON's "Essays." Golden Treasury Series.

HENTZNER — "Itinerarium Germaniae Galliae Angliae, etc." Nuremberg, 1612. 4to.

CRISPIN DE PASS—"Hortus Floridus." Arnhem, 1614.

GERVASE MARKHAM — "The English Husbandman." London, 1614. 4to.

—— "A Way to get Wealth." London, 1638. 4to.

—— "The Country Farm." 1615.

WILLIAM LAWSON—"A New Orchard and Garden." "The Countrie Housewife's Garden." London, 1618. 4to.

De Caux (Solomon)—"Le Jardin de Wilton." London, 1615. Folio.

—— (Isaac)—"Waterworks." London, 1659. Folio.

—— "Les Raisons des Forces." Frankfort, 1615. Folio.

Mollet (André)—"Le Jardin de Plaisir, etc." Stockholm, 1651.

Sir Hugh Platt—"Flora's Paradise." London, 1618. 12mo.

—— "The Garden of Eden." London, 1653. 8vo.

Evelyn—"Kalendarium Hortense." London, 1666. 8vo.

—— "Sylva." London, 1664. Folio.

—— "The Compleat Gardener," etc. 1693. Folio.

—— "Of Gardens; four Books first written in Latin Verse and now made English by J. E." 1673. 8vo (Rapin).

—— Bray's "Memoirs," etc. 1818. 4to.

Boecklern—"Architectura Curiosa Nova." Nuremberg, 1664. Folio.

John Rea—"Flora, Ceres, and Pomona." London, 1665. Folio.

Leonard Meager—"The English Gardener." London, 1670. 4to.

—— "The New Art of Gardening." London, 1697. 12mo.

David Logan—"Oxonia Illustrata." Oxford, 1675. Folio.

—— "Cantabrigia Illustrata." Cambridge, 1688. Folio.

John Worlidge — "Systema Horticulturæ." London, 1677. 8vo.

Sir William Temple — "Miscellanea." "Upon the Gardens of Epicurus." 1685.

Kennett's—"Parochial Antiquities," etc. At the theatre, Oxford, 1695. 4to.

LONDON AND WISE—"The Retired Gard'ner." London, 1706. 8vo.

KIP—"Britannia Illustrata." London, 1709. Folio.

JOHN JAMES—"The Theory and Practice of Gardening, etc., done from the French Original printed at Paris, anno 1709, by John James of Greenwich." London, 1712.

ATKYNS (SIR ROBERT)—"The Ancient and Present State of Gloucestershire." London, 1712.

DUGDALE (SIR WILLIAM)—"Antiquities of Warwickshire." 2 vols. London, 1730.

BADESLADE's "Views." London, 1720. These were apparently made for Harris's "History of Kent," but were also published separately.

STEPHEN SWITZER—"Ichnographia Rustica, or the Nobleman's, Gentleman's, and Gardener's Recreations." London, 1718.

—— "Hydrostatics and Hydraulics." London, 1729. 4to.

JAMES BEEVERELL—"Les Délices de la Grande Bretagne et de l'Irlande." Leyden, 1727.

"The Beauties of Stowe." London, 1746. 8vo.

THOMAS WHEATLY—"Observations on Modern Gardening." 1770.

HORACE WALPOLE—"Essay on Modern Gardening." 1785.

PRICE (SIR UVEDALE)—"An Essay on the Picturesque." London, 1794. 8vo.

—— "On the Decorations near the House."

HUMPHREY REPTON—"Landscape Gardening." London, 1803. Folio.

S. FELTON—"Gleanings on Gardens." London, 1829. 8vo.

ERNEST LAW—"History of Hampton Court Palace."

W. C. HAZLITT—"Gleanings in old Garden Literature." London, 1887.

INDEX